Keto Vegetarian Cookbook

100 easy and tasty recipes to losing extra weight and burning stubborn body fat while keeping your muscles and without going hungry

ZOEY BREANA RIMMER

TABLE OF CONTENTS

INTRODUCTION

"Before starting I want to thank you for purchasing this book. I really hope this book will help you to losing extra weight without going hungry. I would love to receive your feedback with a review on Amazon when you finish. Enjoy the reading."

The fundamentals and how to get started are essential if you're a beginner. Each phase of veganism is defined as shown in this segment. But, first, you should recognize there are three types of vegetarians:

- Lacto-vegetarians enjoy dairy products but eliminate eggs, meat, poultry, and seafood.
- Lacto-Ovo vegetarians will include eggs and dairy but do not prepare poultry, meat, or seafood.
- Vegans avoid seafood, poultry, dairy, eggs, meat, and other animal products (including honey).
- Pescatarians consume seafood; however, they will eliminate poultry and meat products.
- Flexitarians follow a primarily plant-based diet. However, occasionally, they will enjoy meat or other animal products.

It is your choice.

Benefits Of the Vegetarian Diet

You may have chosen one of these reasons for deciding to encompass the vegetarian lifestyle.

- Ethical Reasoning: You possibly hold a personal concern for the welfare of animals, which includes housing them in cages or slaughtering them for food.

- Health-Related Reasoning: You believe that eating meat or other animal products is harmful to your health.

- Environmental Reasoning: You may be concerned about the usage of land and other resources needed to raise livestock.

What the Keto Diet Is & How It Works

A ketogenic diet will assist you with your calorie intake to reduce it below the volume of calories your body can expend in one day. Therefore, you need to summon the energy stored in your fat cells to deliver fuel/energy to your muscles.

The keto diet will limit the volume of carbs you consume. A substantial portion of your daily fuel will come from fat content, which is converted to ketones.

The Process

Ketosis is used to help you drop extra pounds and burn body fat using healthy eating practices. Proteins will fuel your body to burn the fat, which in turn, ketosis will maintain your muscles and make you less hungry.

Your body will remain healthy and work as it should. However, if you don't consume enough carbs from your food, your cells will begin to burn fat for the necessary energy instead. As a result, your body will switch over to ketosis for its energy source as you cut back on your calories and carbs.

Elements of Ketosis: Lipogenesis & Glycogenesis

Two elements that occur when your body doesn't need the glucose:

- **The Stage of Lipogenesis:** If there is a sufficient supply of glycogen in your liver and muscles, any excess is converted to fat and stored.

- **The Stage of Glycogenesis:** The excess of glucose converts to glycogen and is stored in the muscles and liver. Research indicates that only about half of your energy used daily can be saved as glycogen.

When the glycerol and fatty acid molecules are released, the ketogenesis process begins, and acetoacetate is produced. The Acetoacetate is converted to two types of ketone units:

- **Acetone:** This is mostly excreted as waste and can also be metabolized into glucose, which is why individuals on a ketogenic diet will experience a distinctive smelly breath.

- **Beta-hydroxybutyrate or BHB:** Your muscles will convert the acetoacetate into BHB, which will fuel your brain after being on the keto diet for a short time.

Your body will have no more food (similar to when you are sleeping), making your body burn the fat to create ketones. Once the ketones break down the fats, which generate fatty acids, they will burn off in the liver through beta-oxidation.

Thus, when you no longer have a supply of glycogen or glucose, ketosis begins and will use the consumed/stored fat as energy.

The Ketogenic Diet Plans

Flexibility or strictness is the name of the dieting game. Depending on your circumstances, you may not want to have the same goals as another individual. These are the four plans, so you are aware of the different possible levels:

Keto Method 1: The standard ketogenic diet (SKD) consists of high-fat, moderate protein and is low in carbs.

Keto Method 2: The targeted keto diet, also called TKD, will provide you with a technique to add carbs to the diet plan when you are working out.

Keto Method 3: The cyclical ketogenic diet or CKD is observed with five keto days, followed by two high-carbohydrate days.

Keto Method 4: The high-protein keto diet is comparable to the standard keto plan (SKD) in all aspects. However, it does have more protein.

For now, if you are a beginner, you will be using the first method.

Chapter 1: Suggested Foods & Foods to Avoid

Keto Sweetener Options

Favorite Option A: Stevia Drops are offered by *Sweet Leaf* and offer delicious flavors, including hazelnut, vanilla, English toffee, and chocolate. Enjoy making a satisfying cup of sweetened coffee and drinks. However, some individuals think the drops are too bitter. At first, use only three drops to equal one teaspoon of sugar.

Favorite Option B: Xylitol tastes just like sugar! The natural-occurring sugar alcohol has the Glycemic index (GI) standing of 13. If you have tried others and weren't satisfied, this might be for you. Xylitol is also known to keep mouth bacteria in check, which goes a long way to protect your dental health. The ingredient is commonly found in chewing gum. Unfortunately, if used in large amounts, it can cause diarrhea - making chewing gum a laxative if used in large quantities.

- *Urgent Pet Warning*: If you have a puppy in the house, be sure to use caution since it is toxic to dogs (even in small amounts).

Favorite Option C: Swerve Granular Sweetener is also an excellent choice as a blend. It's made from non-digestible carbs sourced from starchy root veggies and select fruits. Give it a try if you don't like the taste of stevia.

Start with ¾ of a teaspoon for every one of sugar. Increase the portion to your liking. Swerve also has its own confectioners/powdered sugar for your baking needs. On the downside, it is more expensive (about twice the price) than other products such as the Pyure. You have to decide if it's worth the difference.

Favorite Option D: The best all-around sweetener is Pyure's Organic All-Purpose Blend with less bitter aftertaste than a stevia-based product. The blend of stevia and erythritol is an excellent alternative to baking, sweetening desserts, and various cooking needs. The substitution ratio is one teaspoon of sugar for each one-third teaspoon of Pyure. Add slowly and adjust to your taste since you can always add a bit more.

If you need powdered sugar, just grind the sweetener in a high-speed blender such as a NutriBullet until it's very dry.

Favorite Option E: Lakanto's Maple-Flavored Syrup is an excellent choice for pancake syrup since it is monk-fruit and erythritol based. Golden Monk Fruit Sweetener also has a brown sugar choice.

The name monk-fruit came from the Buddhist monks over 1,000 years ago and is considered a cooling agent. However, it may not agree with your digestive system, so use it sparingly in baked goods.

Other Pantry Items

These are several items to stock as a vegetarian and also as a vegan. These are just a few items to consider for your specific needs:

- *Beans*: Chickpeas and lentils
- *Coconut Oil*: Versatile uses from roasting veggies to searing tofu or even baking.
- *Dried Fruits*: Dates, dried apricots, and raisins
- *Grains*: White and brown rice, quinoa, millet, faro, and bulgur
- *Tempeh*: This is a great protein source.
- *Nuts*: Cashews, almonds, pine nuts, and pistachios

- *Tofu*: Purchase tofu in blocks.
- *Nutritional Yeast*: Use the yeast to sprinkle on popcorn or potatoes and sauces or tofu coating.
- *Vegetable Stock*: You can purchase veggie stock at the store or make them from scratch.
- *Ground Flax Seeds*: These supply Omega-3 fatty acids
- *Maple Syrup*: As a natural sweetener, it is used for dressing or glazes and is perfect for baking.
- *Miso*: Light and dark paste used soups or for dressings for tofu, veggies, and salad
- *Tahini*: Sesame paste works side by side with miso.

Spices Used

Black Pepper: Pepper promotes nutrient absorption in the tissues all over your body, speeds up your metabolism, and improves digestion. The main ingredient of pepper is a pipeline which gives it a pungent taste. It can boost fat metabolism by as much as 8% for up to several hours after it's ingested. As you will see, it is used throughout your ketogenic recipes.

Cayenne Pepper: The secret ingredient in cayenne is capsaicin, a natural compound that gives the peppers their fiery heat, providing a short increase in your metabolism. The peppers are also rich in vitamins, effective as an appetite controller, smooths out digestion issues, and benefit your heart health.

Cinnamon: Use cinnamon as part of your daily plan to improve your insulin receptor activity. Just put one-half of a teaspoon of cinnamon into a smoothie, shake, or any other keto dessert. As you observe, many of the keto recipes contain the ingredient.

Turmeric: This Asian orange herb dates back to Ayurveda and Chinese medicine. The curcumin, an anti-inflammatory compound found in turmeric, helps improve your insulin receptor function while regulating your blood sugar levels. In addition, it aids in digestion and improves weight management. Add turmeric to your vegetables, green drinks, or smoothies. To maximize the antioxidant elements, add turmeric after the meal has finished cooking.

Italian Seasoning

Combine the following dried fixings to prepare three tablespoons of Italian seasoning:

- Oregano (1 tbsp.)
- Basil (2 tsp.)
- Sage (1 tsp.)
- Thyme - not ground (2 tsp.)
- Rosemary (.5 tsp.)

Heavy Cream Recipe

Here is a simple fix for one cup:

- Mix whole milk (.66 or 2/3 cup)
- With melted butter (.33 or 1/3 cup)

Choose Keto-Friendly Cheese Options
Baked Almond "Feta"
Essential Ingredients:

- Salt (1 tsp.)
- Cloves of garlic (2 minced)
- Olive oil (2.5 tbsp.)
- Water (.5 cup)
- Lemon juice (.25 cup)
- Cheesecloth (3 pieces)

Preparation Steps:

1. Add the salt, minced garlic, olive oil, water, and lemon juice to your blender. Blend well until the results are nice and creamy.
2. Cover a small bowl using the cheesecloth before adding in the blended mixture.
3. Form the cheesecloth into a ball and secure the top.
4. Set the cheese ball into a strainer and place it over the bowl. Let sit for 12 hours or overnight.
5. Ensure your oven is set to 180° Fahrenheit before adding the results from the cheesecloth onto a baking dish that has been greased.
6. Bake for about 42 minutes. Cool and use as desired.

Cashew Cheddar Cheese

Essential Ingredients:
- Raw cashews (.5 cup (+) 2 tbsp.)
- Powdered onion (1 tsp.)
- Sea salt (2 tsp.)
- Unsweetened soy milk (1.75 cups)
- Garlic powder (1 pinch)
- Yeast (.33 cup)
- Agar powder (8 tsp.)
- Lemon juice (1 tbsp.)
- Yellow or white miso (2 tbsp.)
- Canola oil (.25 cup)
- Optional: Truffle oil & chives
- Also Needed: Food processor

Preparation Steps:
1. Brush three to four small ramekins with oil.
2. Add the cashews to the processor. Pulse well.
3. Next, add the salt, powdered onion, garlic powder, and yeast to the processor. Pulse again until combined.
4. Add the agar, oil, and milk to a saucepan. Once the mixture boils, adjust the temperature setting to med-low. Add a lid and simmer (10 min.). Stir as needed to ensure the agar is well dissolved.
5. Scoop the mixture into the food processor and mix steadily until combined (2 min.). Next, blend in the miso, lemon juice, and any additional flavoring ingredients.
6. For sliced or grated cheese, cover the results and refrigerate for 4 hours until firm before removing the "cheese" from the ramekin using a sharp knife.
7. If it is melted cheese that you're after, wait until the "cheese" has hardened and then melt by placing it in a saucepan and heating using medium heat. Mix in additional soy milk to achieve your desired consistency.

8. If covered and refrigerated, the cheese will keep for four days.

Swiss Cheese

Essential Ingredients:
- Powdered agar (1.66 tbsp.)
- Water (1.66 cups)
- Onion flakes (1 tbsp.)
- Yeast (.33 cup)
- Ground dill (.33 tbsp.)
- Soaked cashews (.66 cup)
- Salt (1 pinch)
- Tahini (2 tbsp.)
- Powdered garlic (.33 tbsp.)
- Lemon (1 juiced)
- Dijon mustard (2 tsp.)

Preparation Steps:
1. Oil and set aside a storage container, ramekin, or mold of your choice.
2. Add water, cashews, lemon juice, nutritional yeast, mustard, tahini, garlic, salt, onion flakes, dill, and garlic powder to the blender. Blend until the mixture is completely smooth, occasionally stopping to test for grit. It usually takes anywhere from 1-3 minutes, depending upon your blender.
3. Add one cup of water to a saucepan - wait for it to boil.
4. Slowly whisk in the agar. Let the pot simmer for 10 minutes, whisking as needed to ensure the agar dissolves completely. Add to the blender and mix until creamy.
5. Empty the finished mixture into an oiled container and let cool uncovered in the refrigerator.
6. When cooled - cover and chill for several hours.
7. To make the "Swiss holes," use a plastic straw and poke holes into the cheese using angles at random intervals.
8. Slice and enjoy on sandwiches, crackers, or any other delicious way you choose!

Vegetable Options

This list of veggies is excellent for your lunch or dinner menu plans.

Each of these has the *Net Carbs* listed per 100 grams or 1/2 cup servings:

- Alfalfa Seeds - sprouted (0.2)
- Arugula (2.05)
- Asparagus - 6 spears (2.4)
- Hass Avocado - 0.5 of 1 (1.8)
- Bamboo shoots (3)
- Beans - Green snap (3.6)
- Beet greens (0.63)
- Bell pepper (2.1)
- Broccoli (4.04)
- Cabbage Savoy (3)
- Carrots (6.78)
- Carrots – baby (5.34)
- Cauliflower (2.97)
- Celery (1.37)
- Chard (2.14)
- Chicory greens (0.7)
- Chives (1.85)
- Coriander – Cilantro leaves (0.87)
- Cucumber with peel (3.13)
- Eggplant (2.88)
- Garlic (31)
- Ginger root (15.8)
- Kale (5.15)
- Leeks – bulb (+) lower leaf (12.35)
- Lemongrass – citronella (25.3)
- Lettuce – red leaf (1.36)
- Lettuce – ex. iceberg (1.8)
- Mushrooms - brown (3.7)
- Mustard Greens (1.5)
- Onions – yellow (7.6)

- Onions – scallions or spring (4.7)
- Onions – sweet (6.7)
- Peppers – banana (1.95)
- Peppers – red hot chili (7.3)
- Peppers – jalapeno (3.7)
- Peppers – sweet – green (2.94)
- Peppers – sweet – red (3.9)
- Peppers – sweet – yellow (5.42)
- Portabella mushrooms (2.57)
- Pumpkin (6)
- Radishes (1.8)
- Seaweed – kelp (8.27)
- Seaweed – spirulina (2.02)
- Shiitake mushrooms (4.29)
- Spinach (1.43)
- Squash – crookneck - summer (2.64)
- Squash – winter – acorn (8.9)
- Tomatoes (2.7)
- Turnips (4.6)
- Turnip greens (3.9)
- Summer squash (2.6)
- Raw watercress (3.6)
- White mushrooms (2.3)
- Zucchini (1.5)

Consider These Fruit Sources

Fruits are excellent snack foods. Each of the following is portioned for .5 cup servings or *100 grams*:

- Apples – no skin - boiled – 13.6 total carbs
- Apricots - 7.5 total carbs
- Bananas - 23.4 total carbs
- Fresh Blackberries - 5.4 net carbs
- Fresh Blueberries - 8.2 net carbs
- Fresh Strawberries - 3 net carbs
- Cantaloupe - 6 total carbs
- Raw Cranberries - 4 net carbs

- Gooseberries - 8.8 net carbs
- Kiwi – 14.2 total carbs
- Fresh Boysenberries - 8.8 net carbs
- Oranges – 11.7 total carbs
- Peaches - 11.6 total carbs
- Pears – 19.2 total carbs
- Pineapple - 11 total carbs
- Plums – 16.3 total carbs
- Watermelon - 7.1 total carbs

Note: Please keep in mind, these carb totals are estimated.

Ketogenic Vegetarian Foods To Avoid

You need to be aware of the ones that fall into this category:

- **Processed Polyunsaturated Fats**: Avoid these oils: Sunflower, peanut, grapeseed, sesame, corn, canola, and soybean.

- **Processed Trans Fats**: Avoid fast foods, processed foods, margarine, and commercially prepared baked goods.

Added Sugars: The sugars to avoid include honey, maltose, dextrose, corn syrup, and maltodextrin.

Artificial Sweeteners: Several types to avoid include saccharin, sucralose, and Splenda.

Dairy Products: The ketogenic diet plan uses dairy and dairy products as an essential part of its planning. If you are lactose intolerant, maybe the keto plan isn't for you. It is suggested that you should not drink or consume more than four ounces daily. Instead, choose dairy products that have been cultured and are keto-friendly. Serve and enjoy unsweetened almond milk, hemp milk, or flax milk.

Chapter 2: Breakfast Options

Almonds & Chips Breakfast Cereal

Serving Portions: 1
Total Prep Time: 10 minutes + 4 hours to chill
Macro Nutrients Each Serving:
- Carbs (net): 3 grams
- Calorie Amount: 300
- Protein Counts: 5.9 grams
- Fat Content (total): 27 grams

Essential Ingredients:
- Coconut milk (.25 cup)
- Hemp hearts (3 tbsp.)
- Shredded coconut (.5 tbsp.)
- Chocolate chips (.5 tbsp.)
- Chopped almonds (.5 tbsp.)
- Liquid stevia (1 drop)

Preparation Steps:
1. Combine the fixings in a jar or bowl with a lid.
2. Stir well. Store in the refrigerator for at least four hrs. Overnight is best.
3. Serve it warm or chilled.

Baked Eggs In The Avocado

Serving Portions: 1
Total Prep Time: 20-25 minutes
Macro Nutrients Each Serving:
- Carbs (net): 3 grams
- Calorie Amount: 452
- Protein Counts: 21 grams
- Fat Content (total): 51.5 grams

Essential Ingredients:
- Olive oil (1 tbsp.)
- Avocado (half of 1)
- Egg (1)
- Cheddar cheese - shredded (.5 cup)

Preparation Steps:
1. Warm the oven to reach 425° Fahrenheit/218° Celsius.
2. Discard the avocado pit and remove just enough of the 'insides' to add the egg. Drizzle with the oil and break the egg into the shell.
3. Sprinkle with cheese and bake until the egg is the way you prefer (15-20 min.). Serve.

Breakfast Berry Spread

Serving Portions: 20 - 16 tbsp.
Total Prep Time: 10 minutes
Macro Nutrients Each Serving:
- Carbs (net): 0.5 grams
- Calorie Amount: 20
- Protein Counts: 0.1 grams
- Fat Content (total): 1.8 grams

Essential Ingredients:
- Frozen berries of choice (1 cup - thawed)
- MCT oil (2 tbsp.)
- Psyllium husk powder (1 tsp.)
- Water (1-2 tbsp. or as needed)
- Cinnamon (1 tsp.)

Preparation Steps:
1. Combine each of the fixings and place them into a sealed jar or another container. Add water until the desired texture is acquired. Store the spread in the refrigerator for seven to ten days.
2. Spread the mixture on the toasted bread when it's time to eat.

Breakfast Pizza

Serving Portions: 6
Total Prep Time: 55-60 minutes
Macro Nutrients Each Serving:
- Carbs (net): 5.8 grams
- Calorie Amount: 360
- Protein Counts: 19.2 grams
- Fat Content (total): 34.5 grams

Essential Ingredients:

The Crust:
- Coconut flour (.5 cup)
- Baking soda (.5 tsp.)
- Onion powder (1 tsp.)
- Italian seasoning (2 tsp.)
- Garlic powder (2 tsp.)
- Unsweetened coconut milk (1 cup)
- Flaxseed eggs (6)

The Toppings:
- Olive oil - ex.-virgin (1 tbsp.)
- Baby spinach (3 cups)
- Tomato (half of 1 - sliced thin)
- Flaxseed eggs (3)
- Red pepper flakes (.5 tsp.)

Preparation Steps:

1. Start by making sure your oven is heated to 375° Fahrenheit/191° Celsius.
2. Using parchment paper, cover a large baking sheet
3. Combine the coconut milk, seasonings, and flaxseed egg in a mixing bowl. Whisk well before adding in the coconut flour - combining thoroughly.
4. Evenly spread the dough onto the baking tray before placing it in the heated oven to bake (16 min.).
5. Once the crust has finished cooking, turn the oven temp to 350° Fahrenheit/177° Celsius.

6. Spread the olive oil evenly across the crust before topping with spinach and tomato before topping with red pepper.
7. Put the baking tray back into the oven for approximately 12 minutes.

Brunch Brownies

Serving Portions: 6
Total Prep Time: 20-25 minutes
Macro Nutrients Each Serving:
- Carbs (net): 4.4 grams
- Calorie Amount: 193
- Protein Counts: 7 grams
- Fat Content (total): 14.1 grams

Essential Ingredients:
- Cocoa powder (.25 cup)
- Golden flaxseed meal (1 cup)
- Cinnamon (1 tbsp.)
- Baking powder (.5 tbsp.)
- Salt (.5 tsp.)
- Egg (1 large)
- Coconut oil (2 tbsp.)
- Caramel syrup - Sugar-free (.25 cup)
- Apple cider vinegar (1 tsp.)
- Pumpkin puree (.5 cup)
- Vanilla extract (1 tsp.)
- Slivered almonds (.25 cup)
- Also Needed: Muffin tin with 6 paper liners

Preparation Steps:
1. Warm the oven to reach 350° Fahrenheit/177° Celsius.
2. Line the muffin pan. Mix each of the fixings until well combined. Spoon about ¼ of a cup of the batter into each cup.
3. Sprinkle the almonds over the top of each muffin and press gently.
4. Bake for about 15 minutes.

Brunch Coffee Cake

Serving Portions: 8
Total Prep Time: 30-35 minutes - varies
Macro Nutrients Each Serving:
- Carbs (net): 4.2 grams
- Calorie Amount: 321
- Protein Counts: 13 grams
- Fat Content (total): 28 grams

Essential Ingredients:
The Base:
- Eggs (6 separated)
- Cream cheese (6 oz./170 g)
- Erythritol (.25 cup)
- Liquid stevia (.25 tsp.)
- Unflavored protein powder (.25 cup)
- Cream of tartar (.25 tsp.)
- Vanilla extract (2 tsp.)

The Filling:
- Almond flour (1.5 cups)
- Cinnamon (1 tbsp.)
- Butter (half of a stick)
- Maple syrup substitute (.25 cup)
- Erythritol (.25 cup)
- Also Needed: Dark metal cake pan

Preparation Steps:
1. Warm the oven to reach 325° Fahrenheit/163° Celsius.
2. Separate the egg yolks from the whites. Whisk the yolks with the erythritol.
3. Whisk the tartar and whites of the eggs to create stiff peaks. Then, gently work into the yolks. Mix all of the filling fixings to form the dough.
4. Scoop the batter base into the pan. Top it off with ½ of the cinnamon filling, pushing it down if needed.

5. Bake for 20 minutes. Transfer to the countertop and top the cake off with the remainder of the filling dough.
6. Bake for 20 minutes to half of an hour. Cool for 10 to 20 minutes before serving.

Cauliflower Hash Browns

Serving Portions: 4
Total Prep Time: 40 minutes
Macro Nutrients Each Serving:
- Carbs (net): 5 grams
- Calorie Amount: 282
- Protein Counts: 7 grams
- Fat Content (total): 26 grams

Essential Ingredients:
- Cauliflower (1 lb. or 450 g)
- Eggs (3)
- Yellow onion - grated (half of 1 or 2 oz. or 56 g)
- Salt (1 tsp.)
- Pepper (2 pinches
- For Frying: Butter (4 oz. or 110 g)

Preparation Steps:
1. Rinse and trim the cauliflower. Then, toss it into a food processor or use a box grater to prepare it.
2. Toss the cauliflower into a big mixing container. Add the rest of the fixings and mix. Place it to the side for now (5-10 min.)
3. Warm the oven using a low-temperature setting.
4. Prepare a big, non-stick skillet using a medium-temperature setting to melt a big helping of the butter.
5. Place 3-4 scoops (1 scoop, per pancake) of the cauliflower mixture into the skillet. Gently flatten them until they are circular (about three to four inches or 10 cm in diameter).
6. Fry until lightly browned (4-5 min. each side).
7. Transfer the first batches of pancakes to a baking tray - popping them in the oven to keep warm while making more batches.
8. Add butter to the skillet when needed and adjust the heat to prevent burning. (Note: Use caution not to flip them too quickly, or they will crumble.)

Choco Waffles

Serving Portions: 5
Total Prep Time: 10-15 minutes
Macro Nutrients Each Serving:
- Carbs (net): 3.4 grams
- Calorie Amount: 289
- Protein Counts: 7.2 grams
- Fat Content (total): 26.6 grams

Essential Ingredients:
- Separated eggs (5)
- Coconut flour (4 tbsp.)
- Baking powder (1 tsp.)
- Unsweetened cocoa (.25 cup)
- Granular sweetener (3 tbsp.)
- Melted butter (4.5 oz. or 130 g)
- Milk of choice (3 tbsp.)
- Vanilla (1 tsp.)

Preparation Steps:
1. Whisk the egg whites to form stiff peaks.
2. In another container, whisk the sweetener, baking powder, cocoa with the egg yolks.
3. Slowly mix in the butter to the dry mixture. Next, stir in the vanilla and milk.
4. Stir in the prepared egg whites (small portions at a time).
5. Scoop the mixture into the waffle maker - cook till they're nicely browned to your liking.

Chocolate Muffins

Serving Portions: 6
Total Prep Time: 25-30 minutes
Macro Nutrients Each Serving:
- Carbs (net): 5 grams
- Calorie Amount: 193
- Protein Counts: 7 grams
- Fat Content (total): 14 grams

Essential Ingredients:
- Flaxseed meal (1 cup)
- Sweetened cocoa powder (.25 cup)
- Pumpkin puree (.5 cup)
- Melted coconut oil (.25 cup)
- Water (1.5 cups)
- Muffin tin (6-count)

Preparation Steps:
1. Add the water to the Instant Pot.
2. Whisk each of the fixings in a mixing container.
3. Scoop the batter mixture into the cups - place it on the rack in the cooker.
4. Secure the lid and manually set the time for 18 minutes using the high-pressure setting.
5. Quick-release the pressure and serve.

Coconut Almond Egg Wraps

Serving Portions: 1
Total Prep Time: 10 minutes
Macro Nutrients Each Serving:
- Carbs (net): 3.1 grams
- Calorie Amount: 111
- Protein Counts: 8.1 grams
- Fat Content (total): 7.5 grams

Essential Ingredients:
- Organic eggs (5)
- Coconut flour (1 tbsp.)
- Sea salt (.25 tsp.)
- Almond meal (2 tbsp.)

Preparation Steps:
1. Combine the fixings in a blender and work until creamy.
2. Heat a skillet using the med-high temperature setting.
3. Pour two tablespoons of batter into the pan and cook - covered (3 min.).
4. Flip it over to cook for another three minutes.
5. Serve hot as desired.

Coconut Muesli

Serving Portions: 15
Total Prep Time: 10-15 minutes
Macro Nutrients Each Serving:
- Carbs (net): 2.8 grams
- Calorie Amount: 200
- Protein Counts: 7 grams
- Fat Content (total): 18 grams

Essential Ingredients:
- Sunflower seeds (1 cup)
- Flaked coconut - unsweetened (1 cup)
- Pumpkin seeds (1 cup)
- Pecans (.5 cup)
- Sliced almonds (1 cup)
- Hemp hearts (.5 cup)
- Cinnamon (2 tsp.)
- Vanilla stevia (.25 tsp.)
- Vanilla extract (.5 tsp.)

Preparation Steps:
1. Set the oven to reach 350° Fahrenheit/177° Celsius.
2. Toss each of the fixings - add them to a baking tray.
3. Bake for seven to eight minutes.
4. Let it cool and serve with a glass of almond milk.

Coconut-Walnut Porridge

Serving Portions: 1
Total Prep Time: 10-15 minutes
Macro Nutrients Each Serving:
- Carbs (net): 6 grams
- Calorie Amount: 544
- Protein Counts: 12 grams
- Fat Content (total): 65 grams

Essential Ingredients:
- Coconut milk (.5 cup)
- Almond butter (1 tbsp.)
- Crushed walnuts (3 tbsp.)
- Desiccated coconut (1.5 tbsp.)
- Cinnamon (.25 tsp.)
- Coconut oil (1 tbsp.)

Preparation Steps:
1. Warm the oil, milk, and almond butter in a small saucepan.
2. Once it's boiling, mix in the coconut and walnuts. Mix well and remove from the burner.
3. Let it cool for about five minutes and serve.

Easy Keto Porridge

Serving Portions: 1
Total Prep Time: 15 minutes
Macro Nutrients Each Serving:
- Carbs (net): 5.4 grams
- Calorie Amount: 401
- Protein Counts: 10.1 grams
- Fat Content (total): 22.8 grams

Essential Ingredients:
- Salt (1 pinch)
- Coconut cream (4 tbsp.)
- Psyllium husk powder (1 pinch ground)
- Coconut flour (1 tbsp.)
- Flaxseed Egg (1)
- Coconut butter (1 oz./28 g)

Preparation Steps:
1. Place all of the ingredients in a small pan before placing the pan on the stove on top of a burner set to low heat.
2. Stir the results continuously to encourage porridge to thicken. Continue stirring until your preferred thickness is reached.
3. A small amount of coconut milk or a few berries (fresh or frozen) can also be added to taste.

Egg-Stuffed Avocado

Serving Portions: 2
Total Prep Time: 15 minutes
Macro Nutrients Each Serving:
- Carbs (net): 4.8 grams
- Calorie Amount: 616
- Protein Counts: grams
- Fat Content (total): grams

Essential Ingredients:
- Eggs (4 large)
- Spring onions (2 medium)
- Avocado (1 ex. large)
- Keto-friendly mayonnaise (.25 cup)
- Sour cream/ cream cheese/more mayo (2 tbsp.)
- Dijon mustard (1 tsp.)
- Salt – ex. Pink Himalayan (.25 tsp.)
- Black pepper (as desired)

Preparation Steps:
1. Prepare the Eggs: Add a pinch of salt to help prevent the eggs from cracking to a saucepan filled ¾ full of boiling water. The process should take about ten minutes (for large eggs). Then, drop them in an ice bath to stop the cooking. Peel when cooled
2. Discard the seeds from the avocados, scoop the center, and dice, leaving ½ to one inch of the flesh. Next, slice the onion and dice the eggs.
3. Combine the sour cream, mayonnaise, onion (reserve a bit for the garnish), and Dijon mustard. Give it a sprinkle of pepper and salt if desired. Finally, toss in the freshly cut avocado.
4. Fill each of the avocados and garnish as desired or eat as it is.

French Toast

Serving Portions: 4 slices - 2 per serving
Total Prep Time: 15 minutes
Macro Nutrients Each Serving:
- Carbs (net): 4.9 grams
- Calorie Amount: 242
- Protein Counts: 15.9 grams
- Fat Content (total): 12.9 grams

Essential Ingredients:
- Soft Keto Sandwich Bread (see recipe) or your preferred vegan keto bread (4 slices)
- Non-dairy milk of choice (.5 cup)
- Vanilla protein powder (.25 cup)
- Cinnamon (.25 tsp.)
- Ground nutmeg (1 pinch)

Preparation Steps:
1. Heat a nonstick skillet using a med-low temperature setting.
2. Toast the bread (optional).
3. Whisk the protein powder, cinnamon, and nutmeg with the non-dairy milk until no chunks remain.
4. Soak each piece of bread in the protein powder mixture for about ten seconds total and place them on the frying pan.
5. Wait for around 5 minutes for the bottom to turn golden brown. The mixture on the edges of the bread will be bubbling, and there will be bubbles rising to the surface of the bread. Use that side mixture color as an indicator of how the bottom looks.
6. Flip them and continue cooking on the other side until both sides are golden and toasty (4-5 min.).
7. Top as desired to serve.

High-Protein Yogurt Bowl

Serving Portions: 1
Total Prep Time: 6-7 minutes
Macro Nutrients Each Serving:
- Carbs (net): 9 grams
- Calorie Amount: 274
- Protein Counts: 13 grams
- Fat Content (total): 32.6 grams

Essential Ingredients:
- Almond butter (1 tbsp.)
- Plain yogurt (.5 cup)
- Protein powder (1 tbsp.)
- Sunflower seeds (.5 tbsp.)
- Walnuts (1 tbsp.)
- Chia seeds (.5 tbsp.)
- Coconut milk (.25 cup)

Preparation Steps:
1. Combine the yogurt, coconut milk, and protein powder in the blender.
2. Empty the mixture into a serving dish and add the walnuts, chia seeds, and sunflower seeds. Stir well.
3. Drizzle with the almond oil and serve.

Lemon Waffles

Serving Portions: 4
Total Prep Time: 25-30 minutes
Macro Nutrients Each Serving:
- Carbs (net): 1.8 grams
- Calorie Amount: 99
- Protein Counts: 1.1 grams
- Fat Content (total): 8.2 grams

Essential Ingredients:
- Coconut flour (.25 cup)
- Granulated sweetener (1 tbsp.)
- Salt (1 pinch)
- Whole psyllium husks (1 tbsp.)
- Baking powder (.5 tsp.)
- Melted - coconut butter (2 tbsp.) or coconut oil (1.5 tbsp.)
- Lemon juice (1 tbsp.)
- Nondairy milk of choice (5 tbsp.)
- Vanilla extract (.5 tsp.)

Preparation Steps:
1. Heat a cast-iron pan or ceramic non-stick pan using a med-low temperature setting.
2. Grease the pan with additional coconut oil as needed.
3. Whisk the coconut flour, psyllium, baking powder, and salt. Next, combine with the rest of the fixings in another container.
4. Stir the dry fixings into the wet ones until thoroughly mixed. Let it rest until a stiff dough forms (3-5 min.). Mold this with your hands.
5. Tip: If the coconut oil and psyllium do not absorb enough liquid to form the dough, stir in an additional tablespoon of coconut flour.
6. Divide the dough into four equal portions and shape it into dough balls.
7. Flatten the dough balls and cook for approximately five minutes per side until golden.

8. Let cool for a minute or so before topping.

Maple Cinnamon 'Noatmeal'

Serving Portions: 1
Total Prep Time: 10-15 minutes
Macro Nutrients Each Serving:
- Carbs (net): 4.4 grams
- Calorie Amount: 376
- Protein Counts: 33.7 grams
- Fat Content (total): 23.1 grams

Essential Ingredients:
- Hulled hemp seeds (3 tbsp.)
- Vega Clean Protein in Vanilla/your favorite (3 tbsp.)
- Ground flax seeds (2 tbsp.)
- Cinnamon (.5 tsp.)
- Lakanto sugar-free maple syrup (2 tbsp.)
- Hot water (.75 cup)

Preparation Steps:
1. Combine the dry components in a dish.
2. Whisk and add the water, stirring to thicken as it cools.
3. Top it off with the syrup and serve.

Mushroom Omelet

Serving Portions: 1
Total Prep Time: 10-12 minutes
Macro Nutrients Each Serving:
- Carbs (net): 3 grams
- Calorie Amount: 490
- Protein Counts: 24 grams
- Fat Content (total): 55 grams

Essential Ingredients:
- Egg (1)
- Cheddar (.5 cup)
- Butter (1.5 tbsp.)
- Green onion (1 tbsp.)
- White mushroom (.25 cup)
- Heavy cream (2 tbsp.)

Preparation Steps:
1. Chop the mushrooms and onion.
2. Whisk the heavy cream and egg together with a sprinkle of pepper and salt as desired.
3. Warm a small pan and add butter (½ tbsp.). Toss in the mushroom and sauté them until lightly browned (7 min.).
4. Stir in the whisked egg and cheese.
5. Garnish with the chopped onions and serve.

Onion Tofu

Serving Portions: 3
Total Prep Time: 10-15 minutes
Macro Nutrients Each Serving:
- Carbs (net): 4.7 grams
- Calorie Amount: 184
- Protein Counts: 12.2 grams
- Fat Content (total): 12.7 grams

Essential Ingredients:
- Sliced medium onions (2)
- Tofu blocks (2 into 1-inch cubes)
- Butter (2 tbsp.)
- Grated cheddar cheese (1 cup)
- Freshly cracked black pepper & salt (to your liking)

Preparation Steps:
1. Sprinkle the tofu in a mixing dish with pepper and salt.
2. Scoop the butter into a skillet and add the onions - sauté them (3 min.).
3. Stir in the seasoned tofu and simmer (2 min.).
4. Garnish the mixture using cheese.
5. Place a top on the pot - set on the low heat setting (5 min.).
6. Serve warm.

Pumpkin Pancakes

Serving Portions: 1
Total Prep Time: 20-25 minutes
Macro Nutrients Each Serving:
- Carbs (net): 4 grams
- Calorie Amount: 551
- Protein Counts: 9 grams
- Fat Content (total): 55.7 grams

Essential Ingredients:
- Pumpkin puree (.25 cup)
- Eggs (2)
- Coconut flour (2 tbsp.)
- Cinnamon (.25 tsp.)
- Butter (2 tbsp.)
- Coconut oil (2 tbsp.)
- Vanilla extract (.25 tsp.)

Preparation Steps:
1. Whisk the eggs and puree with the cinnamon and vanilla extract.
2. Slowly add the coconut flour, whisking until the lumps are gone.
3. Warm the oil using a medium-temperature setting.
4. Once the pan is hot, prepare the pancakes until the first side starts to bubble.
5. Flip and continue cooking until golden brown. Serve with butter.

Scallion Pancakes

Serving Portions: 4
Total Prep Time: 20-25 minutes
Macro Nutrients Each Serving:
- Carbs (net): 4.7 grams
- Calorie Amount: 206
- Protein Counts: 3.2 grams
- Fat Content (total): 16.1 grams

Essential Ingredients:
The Cakes:
- Coconut flour (.5 cup)
- Psyllium husk (2 tbsp.)
- Garlic powder (.5 tsp.)
- Salt (.25 tsp.)
- Scallions - white and green parts - sliced into thin rounds (2-3)
- Sesame oil (.25 cup)
- Warm water (1 cup)

The Sauce:
- Rice wine vinegar (1 tsp.)
- Liquid aminos/tamari/soy sauce substitute (1 tbsp.)
- Sesame oil - optional (1 tsp.)
- Water (1 tbsp.)
- Garlic (1 clove)
- Chili flakes (to taste)

Preparation Steps:
1. Warm a bit of oil in a skillet using a med-low heat setting.
2. Finely mince the garlic. Combine the water, oil, garlic, salt, scallions, and warm water. Let the mixture sit for about five minutes for the flavors to mix.
3. In another dish, whisk the coconut flour with the psyllium husks.

4. Slowly add the water to the dry ingredients and let sit for a minute until a dough forms. Then, separate the dough into four equal balls.
5. Flatten one ball in your hands into about a four-inch round. Place on skillet and flatten further with a spatula until it's about six inches in diameter. Fry them until they are golden and crispy (5 min. per side).
6. Repeat until done.
7. For the sauce - whisk the fixings to serve.

Soft Keto Bread - Vegan-Friendly

Serving Portions: 16 slices
Total Prep Time: varies - 2 hours
Macro Nutrients Each Serving:
- Carbs (net): 2 grams
- Calorie Amount: 90
- Protein Counts: 2.8 grams
- Fat Content (total): 5.4 grams

Essential Ingredients:
- Active dry yeast (2.25 tsp. or 1 packet (+) 1 tsp. sugar)
- Warm - not hot - water (1.75 cups)
- Coconut flour (1 cup)
- Psyllium (.5 cup whole husks OR 2 tbsp. (+) 2 tsp. powder)
- Almond butter (.75 cup)
- _Optional_: Salt (1 pinch) if using unsalted almond butter

Preparation Steps:
1. Whisk the yeast and sugar together with ½ of a cup of warm water. Wait for about ten minutes 'to work' until it becomes foamy - resulting in the activation of the yeast.
2. Meanwhile, use a dry fork to whisk the coconut flour and psyllium into a small mixing dish.
3. Stir the yeast mixture (step 1) with the almond butter and one cup of water (reserving the remaining ¼ cup).
4. Combine the dry fixings into the wet, making sure there are no clumps or dry bits. The dough should come together. If there are any dry bits, add in the remaining liquid one to two tablespoons at a time until they are gone. Depending on the type of coconut flour and how humid your climate is, you may not need the extra water.

5. Prepare a baking loaf pan with parchment paper. Arrange the dough in the pan. It won't be smooth.
6. Find a warm, dark place for the dough to rise for 60-90 minutes - until it has increased in size by about 30%. Then, it should 'puff up' and smooth out a bit. While the bread rises, preheat your oven to 350° Fahrenheit/177° Celsius.
7. Once the bread has risen, bake for 50-55 minutes until the crust is hard and hollow sounding. For a thicker crust, continue to bake for another 10 minutes.
8. Transfer the pan from the oven and carefully remove the bread from the pan. Let it cool completely before slicing.
9. Enjoy with any meal or as a quick toasty breakfast side.

Streusel Scones

Serving Portions: 12
Total Prep Time: 35 minutes
Macro Nutrients Each Serving:
- Carbs (net): 3.3 grams
- Calorie Amount: 145
- Protein Counts: 0.6 grams
- Fat Content (total): 11.6 grams

Essential Ingredients:
- Baking powder (1 tsp.)
- Almond flour (2 cups)
- Ground stevia leaf (.25 tsp.)
- Fresh blueberries (1 cup)
- Egg (1)
- Salt (1 pinch)
- Almond milk (2 tbsp.)

The Topping:
- Egg white (1 tbsp.)
- Ground cinnamon (.5 tsp.)
- Slivered almonds (.25 cup.)
- Stevia (1 pinch)

Preparation Steps:
1. Prepare the topping and set it aside.
2. Set the oven temperature to reach 375° Fahrenheit/191° Celsius.
3. Sift or whisk the baking powder with flour, stevia, and salt. Blend in the blueberries.
4. In another container, whisk the egg with the milk until combined. Fold into the dry fixings and shape into 12 scones.
5. Arrange each of the scones on a parchment paper-lined baking tin.
6. Bake until golden brown (20-22 min.)
7. Add the prepared toppings and serve.

Smoothies

Avocado & Almond Milk Smoothie

Serving Portions: 1
Total Prep Time: 10 minutes
Macro Nutrients Each Serving:
- Carbs (net): 4 grams
- Calorie Amount: 587
- Protein Counts: 6 grams
- Fat Content (total): 58 grams

Essential Ingredients:
- Ice cubes (6)
- EZ-Sweetz sweetener (6 drops)
- Unsweetened almond milk (3 oz./85 g)
- Coconut cream (3 oz.)
- Avocado (1)

Preparation Steps:
1. Slice the avocado lengthwise before removing the seeds and the skin.
2. Toss the avocado with the rest of the fixings into the blender.
3. Toss in the ice cubes and blend until the smoothie is creamy smooth.

Blueberry-Banana Bread Smoothies

Serving Portions: 2
Total Prep Time: 8-10 minutes
Macro Nutrients Each Serving:
- Carbs (net): 4.7 grams
- Calorie Amount: 270
- Protein Counts: 3 grams
- Fat Content (total): 23 grams

Essential Ingredients:
- Chia seeds (1 tbsp.)
- Golden flaxseed meal (3 tbsp.)
- Vanilla unsweetened coconut milk (2 cups)
- Blueberries (.25 cup)
- Liquid stevia (10 drops)
- MCT oil (2 tbsp.)
- Xanthan gum (.25 tsp.)
- Banana extract (1.5 tsp.)
- Ice cubes (2-3)

Preparation Steps:
1. Combine all of the ingredients into a blender.
2. Wait a few minutes for the seeds and flax to absorb some of the liquid.
3. Pulse for one to two minutes until well combined and the texture you choose. Lastly, add the ice to your preference.

Cherry Coconut Smoothies

Serving Portions: 2
Total Prep Time: 8-10 minutes
Macro Nutrients Each Serving:
- Carbs (net): 1.6 grams
- Calorie Amount: 80
- Protein Counts: 1.7 grams
- Fat Content (total): 1.8 grams

Essential Ingredients:
- Cherries (1 cup)
- Almond milk (.5 cup)
- Ice (1 cup)
- Coconut water (.5 cup)

Preparation Steps:
1. Remove the pits from the cherries.
2. Toss each of the fixings into a blender and pulse till it's incorporated and smooth.

Chocolate Smoothie

Serving Portions: 1 large
Total Prep Time: 5-6 minutes
Macro Nutrients Each Serving:
- Carbs (net): 4.4 grams
- Calorie Amount: 570
- Protein Counts: 34.5 grams
- Fat Content (total): 46 grams

Essential Ingredients:
- Large eggs (2)
- Extra-virgin coconut oil (1 tbsp.)
- Almond or Coconut butter (1.5 to 2 tbsp.)
- Coconut milk or heavy whipping cream (.25 cup)
- Chia seeds (1-2 tbsp.)
- Cinnamon (.5 tsp.)
- Stevia extract (3-5 drops)
- Plain or chocolate whey protein (.25 cup)
- Unsweetened cacao powder (1 tbsp.)
- Water (.25 cup)
- Vanilla extract (.5 tsp.)
- Ice (.5 cup)

Preparation Steps:
1. Break the eggs along with the rest of the fixings into the blender.
2. Pulse until frothy.
3. Add to a chilled glass to serve.

Cinnamon Smoothie

Serving Portions: 1
Total Prep Time: 4-5 minutes
Macro Nutrients Each Serving:
- Carbs (net): 4.7 grams
- Calorie Amount: 467
- Protein Counts: 23.6 grams
- Fat Content (total): 40.3 grams

Essential Ingredients:
- Cinnamon (.5 tsp.)
- Coconut milk (.5 cup)
- Water (.5 cup)
- Extra-Virgin coconut or MCT oil (1 tbsp.)
- Chia seeds - ground (1 tbsp.)
- Plain or vanilla whey protein (.25 cup)
- Stevia drops - optional (as desired)

Preparation Steps:
1. Pour the milk, cinnamon, protein powder, and chia seeds into a blender.
2. Empty the coconut oil, ice, and water. Add a few drops of stevia if desired.

Lean & Green Breakfast Smoothie - Vegan-Friendly

Serving Portions: 1
Total Prep Time: 3-5 minutes
Macro Nutrients Each Serving:
- Carbs (net): 9.5 grams
- Calorie Amount: 650
- Fat Content (total): 50 grams

Essential Ingredients:
- Avocado (half of 1)
- Cucumber (1/3 of 1)
- Spinach (2 cups)
- Coconut milk (6 oz./170 g)
- Almond milk - unsweetened (6 oz.)
- Matcha powder (1 tsp.)
- Lime - juice only (half of 1)
- Low-sugar vanilla protein powder (half of 1 scoop)
- To Garnish: Chia seeds (.5 tsp.)

Preparation Steps:
1. Place spinach and coconut milk in a blender, blitz to break down spinach to make room for other ingredients.
2. Add all other ingredients and blend until smooth.

Melon Green Tea Smoothies

Serving Portions: 2
Total Prep Time: 8-10 minutes
Macro Nutrients Each Serving:
- Carbs (net): 2.5 grams
- Calorie Amount: 247
- Protein Counts: 4.5 grams
- Fat Content (total): 5.4 grams

Essential Ingredients:
- Brewed green tea (1 cup)
- Cantaloupe (1 cup)
- Pear (1)
- Frozen pineapple chunks (1 cup)
- Plain Greek yogurt (.5 cup)
- Fresh mint (4 leaves + additional to taste)

Preparation Steps:
1. Remove the core from the pear. Cut the pear, cantaloupe, and pineapple into chunks.
2. Combine tea with pineapple, cantaloupe, pear, yogurt, and mint leaves in a blender.
3. Mix until they are smooth and serve in two chilled glasses.

Mixed Berry Smoothie

Serving Portions: 1
Total Prep Time: 6 minutes **
Macro Nutrients Each Serving:
- Carbs (net): 7 grams
- Calorie Amount: 400
- Protein Counts: 7.4 grams
- Fat Content (total): 41 grams

Essential Ingredients:
- Ice cubes (6)
- Your choice of sweetener (to taste)
- Coconut milk (.33 cup)
- Mixed berries (.5 cup - frozen)
- Water (.5 cup)
- Olive oil - ex. virgin (1 tbsp.)

Preparation Steps:
1. Cream the coconut milk: **Put the can of coconut milk in the refrigerator overnight. The next morning, open the can and spoon out the coconut milk that has solidified. _Don't shake the can before opening it._ Discard the liquids.
2. Add all of the ingredients, save the ice cubes to the blender - blend on using the low-speed setting until it's pureed. Thin with water as needed.
3. Add in the ice cubes and blend until the smoothie reaches your desired consistency.

Mocha Smoothies

Serving Portions: 3
Total Prep Time: 4-5 minutes
Macro Nutrients Each Serving:
- Carbs (net): 4 grams
- Calorie Amount: 176
- Protein Counts: 3 grams
- Fat Content (total): 16 grams

Essential Ingredients:
- Avocado (1)
- Coconut milk – from the can (.5 cup)
- Unsweetened almond milk (1.5 cups)
- Instant coffee crystals – regular or decaffeinated (2 tsp.)
- Vanilla extract (1 tsp.)
- Erythritol blend/granulated stevia (3 tbsp.)
- Unsweetened cocoa powder (3 tbsp.)

Preparation Steps:
1. Slice the avocado in half. Discard the pit and remove most of the center. Add it along with the rest of the fixings into a blender.
2. Mix until it's like you like it. Serve in three chilled glasses.

Raspberry-Chocolate Cheesecake Smoothie

Serving Portions: 1
Total Prep Time: 4-5 minutes
Macro Nutrients Each Serving:
- Carbs (net): 7 grams
- Calorie Amount: 512
- Protein Counts: 6.89 grams
- Fat Content (total): 54 grams

Essential Ingredients:
- Frozen or fresh raspberries (.33 cup)
- Coconut milk/heavy whipping cream (.25 cup)
- Full-fat cream cheese/creamed coconut milk (.25 cup)
- Unsweetened cacao powder (1 tbsp.)
- Coconut oil - ex.-virgin preferred (1 tbsp.)
- Water (.5 cup)
- Optional: Liquid stevia extract (3-5 drops)

Preparation Steps:
1. Place all of the goodies for your smoothie in a blender.
2. Blend it until frothy and serve in a chilled glass.

Spinach & Cucumber Smoothies

Serving Portions: 2
Total Prep Time: 8 minutes
Macro Nutrients Each Serving:
- Carbs (net): 3 grams
- Calorie Amount: 330
- Protein Counts: 10.1 grams
- Fat Content (total): 32.4 grams

Essential Ingredients:
- Ice cubes (6)
- Sweetener of choice (to taste)
- Coconut milk (.75 cup)
- MCT oil (2 tbsp.)
- Cucumber (2.5 oz./70 g)
- Spinach (2 handfuls)
- Coconut milk (1 cup)
- Xanthan gum (.25 tsp.)

Preparation Steps:
1. Cream the coconut milk: Put the can of coconut milk in the fridge overnight. The next morning, open the can and spoon out the coconut milk that has solidified. Don't shake the can before opening the can. Discard the liquids.
2. Add all of the ingredients (save the ice cubes) to the blender - mix using the low speed until pureed. Thin with water as needed.
3. Add in the ice cubes and blend until the smoothie reaches your desired consistency.

Healthy Beverages

Eggnog - Keto - Vegan-Friendly

Serving Portions: 4
Total Prep Time: 5-6 minutes
Macro Nutrients Each Serving:
- Carbs (net): 2.2 grams
- Calorie Amount: 269
- Protein Counts: 8.2 grams
- Fat Content (total): 25.7 grams

Essential Ingredients:
- Unsweetened non-dairy milk or water (3 cups)
- Raw - unsalted pecans (1 cup)
- Vanilla protein powder (.25 cup)
- Granulated sweetener - ex. "golden" variety (2 tbsp.)
- Ground nutmeg (1 tsp.)
- Cinnamon or allspice (1 pinch)
- Salt (1 pinch)
- Vanilla extract (1 tsp.)

Preparation Steps:
1. Using a high-speed blender, puree the fixings until completely smooth (approx. 1.5 minutes). Start off using the low setting and work up to high for the last 30 seconds.
2. If you want the eggnog to be super smooth, you can strain it using a nut-milk bag.
3. Serve chilled or warm it on the stove to a tasty treat.

Hot Chocolate

Serving Portions: 1
Total Prep Time: 4-5 minutes
Macro Nutrients Each Serving:
- Carbs (net): 1 gram
- Calorie Amount: 216
- Protein Counts: 1 gram
- Fat Content (total): 23 grams

Essential Ingredients:
- Cocoa powder (1 tbsp.)
- Unsalted butter (1 oz./28 g)
- Boiling water (1 cup)
- Powdered erythritol - optional (1 tsp.)
- Vanilla extract (.25 tsp.)
- Also Needed: Immersion blender

Preparation Steps:
1. Add each of the ingredients into a tall container to prepare using the blender. Mix for about 15 to 20 seconds until the foam is no longer on the top.
2. Pour the cocoa into the cups and serve.

Pumpkin Spice Latte

Serving Portions: 1
Total Prep Time: 5 minutes
Macro Nutrients Each Serving:
- Carbs (net): 1 gram
- Calorie Amount: 216
- Protein Counts: 0.5 grams
- Fat Content (total): 23 grams

Essential Ingredients:
- Boiling water (1 cup)
- Pumpkin pie spice ** (1 tsp.)
- Unsalted butter (1 oz./28 g)
- Instant coffee powder (1-2 tsp)
- Suggested: Immersion blender

Preparation Steps:
1. Combine the instant coffee, spices, and butter in a mixing dish.
2. Add the water and blend for 20 to 30 seconds until foamy.
3. Pour into the cup and sprinkle with the spice.
4. Top it off with a scoop of whipped cream if desired to serve.
5. Note: You can also use cinnamon if you do not have pumpkin spice.

Shamrock Shake

Serving Portions: 1
Total Prep Time: 5 minutes
Macro Nutrients Each Serving:
- Carbs (net): 5 grams
- Calorie Amount: 352
- Protein Counts: 24.9 grams
- Fat Content (total): 24.5 grams

Essential Ingredients:
- Vanilla protein powder of choice - ex.- Vega Sport (.25 cup)
- Fresh spinach** (2 cups or less/as desired)
- Fresh mint leaves** (.25 cup)
- Mashed avocado OR full-fat canned coconut milk (.5 cup)
- Nondairy milk of choice (1 cup) OR Ice cubes (2 cups for a thicker drink)

Preparation Steps:
1. **Loosely pack the mint and spinach.
2. Prepare a high-speed blender with all of the fixings.
3. Pulse until creamy smooth.

Turmeric Milk

Serving Portions: 1
Total Prep Time: Under 15 minutes
Macro Nutrients Each Serving:
- Carbs (net): 2.3 grams
- Calorie Amount: 143
- Protein Counts: 1.5 grams
- Fat Content (total): 2.9 grams

Essential Ingredients:
- Fresh turmeric & ginger root (1.5-inch piece each)
- Honey (1 tbsp.)
- Unsweetened almond milk (1 cup)
- Optional: Ground turmeric & ginger (1 pinch each)

Preparation Steps:
1. Peel, grate and toss the turmeric and ginger root with the honey in a mixing container.
2. Warm the milk in a saucepan using a med-low temperature setting. Once small bubbles begin to form around the edges, adjust the temperature to low.
3. Transfer about two tablespoons of milk to the turmeric mixture - allowing it to soften and melt into a paste-like mixture.
4. Mix the turmeric paste into milk in the saucepan. Adjust the temperature setting to med-low - simmer till the mix is thoroughly combined. Blend it using an immersion blender for a smooth texture.
5. Pour the turmeric tea into a mug and top with ground turmeric and cinnamon.

Vanilla Coffee & Whipped Cream

Serving Portions: 1
Total Prep Time: 5-6 minutes
Macro Nutrients Each Serving:
- Carbs (net): 2 grams
- Calorie Amount: 206
- Protein Counts: 2 grams
- Fat Content (total): 21 grams

Essential Ingredients:
- Heavy whipping cream (.25 cup)
- Coffee (1 cup prepared)
- Vanilla extract (.25 tsp.)
- Optional Garnish: Cocoa powder or Ground cinnamon

Preparation Steps:
1. Prepare your coffee as you normally do without the extras.
2. Briskly whisk the vanilla and cream to form soft peaks.
3. Pour the coffee into a large mug with a dollop of cream.
4. Sprinkle with a dusting of cinnamon or cocoa powder to your liking.
5. Serve and enjoy with a portion of nuts for a healthy snack.

Chapter 3: Lunch & Dinner Salad - Pasta & Sauce Options

Bread Twists

Serving Portions: 10
Total Prep Time: 30 minutes
Macro Nutrients Each Serving:
- Carbs (net): 1 gram
- Calorie Amount: 204
- Protein Counts: 7 grams
- Fat Content (total): 18 grams

Essential Ingredients:
- Almond flour (.5 cup)
- Coconut flour (4 tbsp.)
- Salt (.5 tsp.)
- Baking powder (1 tsp.)
- Shredded cheese - your choice (1.5 cups)
- Butter (2.33 oz./66 g)
- Egg (2 - Use 1 for brushing the tops)
- Green pesto (2 oz./56 g)

Preparation Steps:

1. Warm the oven to reach 350° Fahrenheit/177° Celsius.
2. Prepare a baking tray using a layer of parchment baking paper.
3. Whisk together each of the dry fixings.
4. Use the low heat setting to melt the butter and cheese together. Stir until smooth and add the egg. Stir well.
5. Combine all of the fixings to make the dough.
6. Place and roll the dough between two layers of parchment baking paper until it's about one inch thick. Remove the top sheet.
7. Spread the pesto on top of the dough and slice it into one-inch strips.
8. Twist the dough and arrange it on the baking tin.
9. Brush the twists with the second egg (gently whisked).
10. Bake until they're nicely brown as desired (15-20 min.).

Salad Favorites

Asian Zucchini Salad

Serving Portions: 1
Total Prep Time: 25-30 minutes
Macro Nutrients Each Serving:
- Carbs (net): 7 grams
- Calorie Amount: 846
- Protein Counts: 14 grams
- Fat Content (total): 85.5 grams

Essential Ingredients:
- Medium zucchini (1)
- Sesame oil (1.5 tbsp.)
- Shredded cabbage (.5 cup)
- Sunflower seeds (1.5 tbsp.)
- Almonds (.5 tbsp.)
- White vinegar (1 tbsp.)
- Crumbled feta cheese (.5 cup)

Preparation Steps:
1. Roast the almonds in a deep-frying pan using a low-temperature setting. (Whole almonds: 325° Fahrenheit/163° Celsius oven for 5-15 minutes. Or, sliced about 5-10 minutes).
2. Use a spiralizer to shred the zucchini into strips.
3. Prepare the salad using cabbage, zucchini, almonds, and sunflower seeds.
4. Whisk both oils and the vinegar and spritz over the salad.
5. Garnish with the feta and toss before serving.

Caprese Salad

Serving Portions: 4
Total Prep Time: 40 minutes
Macro Nutrients Each Serving:
- Carbs (net): 4.6 grams
- Calorie Amount: 191
- Protein Counts: 7.7 grams
- Fat Content (total): 63.5 grams

Essential Ingredients:
- Grape tomatoes (3 cups)
- Peeled garlic cloves (4)
- Avocado oil (2 tbsp.)
- Mozzarella balls (10 pearl-sized)
- Fresh basil leaves (.25 cup)
- Baby spinach leaves (4 cups)
- Brine reserved from the cheese (1 tbsp.)
- Pesto (1 tbsp.)

Preparation Steps:
1. Warm the oven to reach 400° Fahrenheit/204° Celsius.
2. Prepare a baking tin with a layer of aluminum foil.
3. Arrange the tomatoes and cloves in the prepared pan. Spritz with the oil. Bake until the tops are slightly browned (20-30 min.).
4. Drain the liquid (saving 1 tbsp.) from the brine. Then, mix the pesto with the brine.
5. Arrange the spinach in a large salad container. Transfer the tomatoes to the dish along with the roasted garlic. Drizzle with the pesto sauce.
6. Garnish with the mozzarella balls and freshly torn basil leaves.

Cauliflower & Pine Nut Salad

Serving Portions: 1
Total Prep Time: 2 hours 15 minutes
Macro Nutrients Each Serving:
- Carbs (net): 8 grams
- Calorie Amount: 638
- Protein Counts: 10 grams
- Fat Content (total): 63.4 grams

Essential Ingredients:
- Cauliflower (.25 cup)
- Onion leeks (2 tbsp.)
- Pine nuts (.25 cup)
- Sour cream (2 tbsp.)
- Iceberg lettuce (.5 cup)
- Mayonnaise (.25 cup)
- Feta cheese (.25 cup)

Preparation Steps:
1. Chop the cauliflower, onion, and pine nuts. Shred the lettuce.
2. Toast the pine nuts using the medium heat setting.
3. Combine all of the fixings in a large container and place them in the fridge for a minimum of two hours.
4. Serve cold.

Corn-Avocado Salad

Serving Portions: 4
Total Prep Time: 10 minutes
Macro Nutrients Each Serving:
- Carbs (net): 4.5 grams
- Calorie Amount: 147
- Protein Counts: 3.5 grams
- Fat Content (total): 11 grams

Essential Ingredients:
The Salad:
- Cooked - corn on the cob - husk removed (1)
- Romaine head (1 chopped)
- Quartered grape tomatoes (4)
- Sliced red onion (.25 cup)
- Sliced avocado (half of 1)

The Dressing:
- Minced shallots (1 tbsp.)
- Dijon mustard (2 tsp.)
- 1% Vegan buttermilk (6 tbsp.)
- White wine vinegar (2 tbsp.)
- Garlic powder (.25 tsp.)
- Kosher salt (.5 tsp.)
- Black pepper (1 pinch)
- Olive oil - ex.-virgin (2 tbsp.)

Preparation Steps:
1. Whisk each of the dressing ingredients and place them in a serving jar.
2. Combine the salad fixings in a big mixing container and toss with the dressing.

Feta Cheese Salad With Balsamic Butter

Serving Portions: 1
Total Prep Time: 25-30 minutes
Macro Nutrients Each Serving:
- Carbs (net): 8 grams
- Calorie Amount: 609
- Protein Counts: 16 grams
- Fat Content (total): 69.6 grams

Essential Ingredients:
- Crumbled feta cheese (.5 cup)
- Pumpkin seeds (.125 cup)
- Butter (.25 cup)
- Balsamic vinegar (1 tbsp.)
- Baby spinach (.5 cup)

Preparation Steps:
1. Warm the oven to reach 400° Fahrenheit/204° Celsius.
2. Crumble the cheese on a greased baking tray. Bake for about 10 minutes.
3. Use the high-temperature setting on the stovetop to heat a dry skillet. Toast the seeds until they begin to pop.
4. Reduce the temperature and add the butter. Simmer until golden brown and add the vinegar. Simmer for about two minutes and turn off the burner.
5. Arrange the baby spinach leaves on a salad dish. Pour the butter over that and top it with the feta cheese before serving.

Greek Salad

Serving Portions: 1
Total Prep Time: 8-10 minutes
Macro Nutrients Each Serving:
- Carbs (net): 8 grams
- Calorie Amount: 594
- Protein Counts: 12 grams
- Fat Content (total): 57.5 grams

Essential Ingredients:
- Red onion (.25 cup)
- Tomato (.25 cup)
- Cucumber (.25 cup)
- Bell pepper (.25 cup)
- Feta cheese (.5 cup)
- Olives (1 tbsp.)
- Vinegar - red wine (.5 tbsp.)
- Olive oil (3 tbsp.)

Preparation Steps:
1. Dice the tomato, chop the olives, and slice the onion, cucumber, and pepper. Combine the bell pepper with the tomato, cucumber, crumbled feta cheese, and onion.
2. Spritz using the oil and vinegar with a shake of pepper and salt to your liking.
3. Toss until all of the ingredients are well mixed before serving.

Grilled Vegetable Salad with Feta

Serving Portions: 4 large
Total Prep Time: 55 minutes
Macro Nutrients Each Serving:
- Carbs (net): 8 grams
- Calorie Amount: 186
- Protein Counts: 5 grams
- Fat Content (total): 14 grams

Essential Ingredients:
- Zucchini & eggplant (1 medium - each)
- Garlic (2 minced cloves)
- Red bell pepper (1)
- Olive oil - ex. virgin (3 tbsp.)
- Sea salt (.75 tsp.)
- Crumbled feta (.5 tsp.)
- Dried oregano (.5 tsp.)
- Cracked black pepper (.5 tsp.)

Preparation Steps:
1. Heat the grill ahead of time using a medium setting.
2. Slice the zucchini and eggplant into ¼-inch segments and the pepper into ½-inch pieces.
3. Arrange the veggies on the grill and cook for about three to four minutes per side.
4. Place the vegetables on a chopping block for a few minutes to cool. Chop into ½-inch bits and add to a serving container of choice. Blend in the garlic, oil, pepper, salt, and oregano, tossing well to evenly coat. Sprinkle it using cheese and toss again.
5. Note: You can add salt to the eggplant slices about ½ hour before they are cooked to reduce some of the bitter taste.

Healthy Salad In a Jar

Serving Portions: 1
Total Prep Time: 10 minutes
Macro Nutrients Each Serving:
- Carbs (net): 4 grams
- Calorie Amount: 215
- Protein Counts: 8.1 grams
- Fat Content (total): 18.7 grams

Essential Ingredients:
- Black pepper & salt (as desired)
- Keto-friendly mayonnaise (4 tbsp.)
- Scallion (half of 1)
- Cucumber (.25 oz./7 g)
- Red bell pepper (.25 oz.)
- Cherry tomatoes (.25 oz.)
- Leafy greens (.25 oz.)
- Seasoned tempeh (4 oz./110 g)

Preparation Steps:
1. Chop or shred the vegetables as desired. Layer in the dark leafy greens first, followed by the onions, tomato, bell peppers, avocado, and shredded carrot.
2. Top with the tempeh or use the same amount of another high-protein option to mix things up in later weeks.
3. Top with keto-vegan mayonnaise before serving.

Keto Salad Nicoise

Serving Portions: 1
Total Prep Time: 25-30 minutes
Macro Nutrients Each Serving:
- Carbs (net): 8 grams
- Calorie Amount: 544
- Protein Counts: 18 grams
- Fat Content (total): 48.4 grams

Essential Ingredients:
- Large egg (1)
- Olive oil (2 tbsp.)
- Chopped celery (.5 cup)
- Snow peas (.5 cup)
- Garlic (.25 tbsp.)
- Shredded romaine lettuce (1 cup)
- Chopped green onion (.5 tbsp.)
- Chopped olives (.5 tbsp.)
- Crumbled feta cheese (.5 cup)
- Balsamic vinegar (1 tbsp.)

Preparation Steps:
1. Hard boil the egg and remove the peel when cooled.
2. Add olive oil to a small pan. Chop and sauté the garlic, olives, and snow peas until the peas are bright green.
3. Prepare a big salad container and add the cooked veggies, lettuce, celery, and green onion.
4. Make the dressing by whisking the oil and vinegar with pepper and salt.
5. Combine the fixings and toss well before serving.

Lemon Tahini Courgette Salad

Serving Portions: 6
Total Prep Time: 20 minutes
Macro Nutrients Each Serving:
- Carbs (net): 11 grams
- Calorie Amount: 110
- Protein Counts: 7 grams
- Fat Content (total): 12 grams

Essential Ingredients:
- Artichoke hearts - in water (2 cans @ 14 oz. or 400 g each)
- Chickpeas (14 oz. can)
- Cherry tomatoes - halved (1 pint)

The Dressing:
- Dijon mustard (1 tbsp.)
- Tahini (1 tbsp.)
- Garlic powder (.5 tsp.)
- Lemon juice (2 tbsp. of fresh squeezed/1 large)
- Pure keto-friendly maple syrup or substitute (1 tsp.)
- Black pepper & salt (.25 tsp. each)

Preparation Steps:
1. Gently squeeze each of the artichoke hearts over the sink to release any excess juice - roughly chop them.
2. Slice and quarter the courgettes and cut the cherry tomatoes into halves. Zest the lemon.
3. Rinse and drain the chickpeas in a colander.
4. Add the tomatoes, zucchini, artichokes, and chickpeas into a big mixing container.
5. Toss and whisk the dressing fixings till the mixture is smooth. (Add up to one tablespoon of water if the sauce is too thick.)
6. Pour the sauce over the veggies in the mixing container - tossing until all the fixings are evenly coated with the delicious dressing. Garnish using the desired amount of lemon zest.

7. Serve the salad promptly if desired. You can also place it in the refrigerator if you enjoy it cold and chill for ½ hour until ready to serve.
8. Enjoy anytime as a meal or portioned for a snack! It is delicious - either way!

Salad Sandwich

Serving Portions: 1
Total Prep Time: 6-8 minutes
Macro Nutrients Each Serving:
- Carbs (net): 4.5 grams
- Calorie Amount: 104
- Protein Counts: 4.3 grams
- Fat Content (total): 14.7 grams

Essential Ingredients:
- Butter (.5 oz./14 g)
- Romaine or baby gem lettuce (2 oz./56 g)
- Adam cheese (1 oz./28 g)
- Cherry tomato (1 sliced)
- Sliced avocado (half of 1)

Preparation Steps:
1. Rinse the lettuce and slice the rest of the ingredients.
2. Add butter on the leaves with a layer of cheese, avocado, and tomato. Top it off with lettuce and serve.

Pasta Favorites

Baked Zucchini Noodles With Feta

Serving Portions: 3
Total Prep Time: 20 minutes
Macro Nutrients Each Serving:
- Carbs (net): 5 grams
- Calorie Amount: 105
- Protein Counts: 4 grams
- Fat Content (total): 8 grams

Essential Ingredients:
- Plum tomato (1 - quartered)
- Spiralized zucchini (2)
- Feta cheese (8 cubes)
- Pepper and salt (1 tsp. of each)
- Olive oil (1 tbsp.)

Preparation Steps:
1. Grease a roasting pan. Set the oven temperature at 375° Fahrenheit/191° Celsius.
2. Prepare the noodles with a spiralizer and add to the prepared pan with olive oil and tomatoes. Lightly dust with pepper and salt.
3. Bake for 10-15 minutes.
4. Transfer from the oven and add the cheese cubes, tossing to combine before serving.

Brussels Sprouts Spaghetti

Serving Portions: 1
Total Prep Time: 10-15 minutes
Macro Nutrients Each Serving:
- Carbs (net): 5 grams
- Calorie Amount: 259
- Protein Counts: 7 grams
- Fat Content (total): 23 grams

Essential Ingredients:
- Shirataki noodles (1 pkg.)
- Brussels sprouts (.25 cup)
- Garlic (1 clove)
- Cream cheese - vegan-friendly suggested (2 tbsp.)
- Olive oil (1 tbsp.)
- Black pepper and salt (as desired)
- Nutritional yeast (1 tbsp.)

Preparation Steps:
1. Pour the oil into a skillet to get hot.
2. Shred the sprouts and add to the pan with the garlic. Sauté to soften for a few minutes.
3. Rinse and drain the noodles and combine with the rest of the fixings.
4. Stir every few minutes until it's creamy, only adding small amounts of water (no more than 1 tbsp.) at a time.
5. Combine well and serve.

Coconut Lime Noodles With Chili Tamari Tofu

Serving Portions: 4
Total Prep Time: 60 minutes
Macro Nutrients Each Serving:

- Carbs (net): 5.5 grams
- Calorie Amount: 374
- Protein Counts: 16 grams
- Fat Content (total): 31 grams

Essential Ingredients:

The Noodles:

- Full-fat coconut milk (13.5 oz./380 g can)
- Shirataki noodles (8 oz./226 g each/2 pkg.)
- Sesame seeds (4 tbsp.)
- Juice and zest (1 lime)
- Ground or freshly grated ginger (.5 tsp.)
- Red pepper flakes (.25 tsp.)
- Salt (1 pinch)

The Tofu:

- Olive oil (1 tbsp.)
- Extra-firm tofu (13.5 oz./380 g/1 block)
- Low-sodium tamari (4 tbsp.)
- Cayenne pepper (.25 tsp.)

Preparation Steps:

1. Warm the oven to reach 350° Fahrenheit/177° Celsius.
2. Drain the tofu. Press out the excess moisture. Cube into roughly 1x1-inch blocks.
3. Mix the oil, cayenne, and tamari. Toss the tofu cubes in a single layer using a shallow container. Pour the mixture over the tofu. Flip the pieces several times until they're evenly coated.
4. Arrange the tofu pieces on a baking tray and set a timer to bake for 20 to 25 minutes.

5. Meanwhile, drain and rinse the noodles. Add to a pan using medium heat, with the rest of the noodle fixings. Mix until combined.
6. Offset the lid and simmer for about ten minutes. Then, lower the temperature setting to simmer for an additional ten minutes.
7. When ready, turn off the heat under the noodles. Cool for a few minutes before plating.
8. Garnish using red pepper flakes, microgreens, lime zest, or more sesame seeds.

Edamame Kelp Noodles

Serving Portions: 2
Total Prep Time: 10-12 minutes
Macro Nutrients Each Serving:
- Carbs (net): 4.9 grams
- Calorie Amount: 139
- Protein Counts: 7.8 grams
- Fat Content (total): 8.6 grams

Essential Ingredients:
- Kelp noodles (1 pkg.)
- Shelled edamame (.5 cup)
- Julienned carrots (.25 cup)
- Sliced mushrooms (.25 cup)
- Frozen spinach (1 cup)

The Sauce:
- Sesame oil (1 tbsp.)
- Tamari (2 tbsp.)
- Ground ginger (.5 tsp.)
- Garlic powder (.5 tsp.)
- Sriracha (.25 tsp.)

Preparation Steps:
1. Soak the noodles in water. Drain well.
2. Use the medium heat setting and place the sauce fixings in a saucepan. Add the veggies and warm.
3. Stir in the noodles and simmer for two to three minutes, stirring occasionally.

Lo Mein - Vegan-Friendly

Serving Portions: 1 large
Total Prep Time: 15-20 minutes
Macro Nutrients Each Serving:
- Carbs (net): 4.4 grams
- Calorie Amount: 195
- Protein Counts: 5.1 grams
- Fat Content (total): 13.9 grams

Essential Ingredients:
- Kelp noodles (1 pkg./as desired)
- Shredded carrots (2 tbsp.)
- Frozen broccoli (1 cup)

The Sauce:
- Tamari (2 tbsp.)
- Sesame oil (1 tbsp.)
- Garlic powder (.5 tsp.)
- Ground ginger (.5 tsp.)
- Sriracha/your preference chili pepper (.25 tsp.)

Preparation Steps:
1. Open the noodles to soak them in water.
2. Prepare a saucepan using the med-low temperature setting, toss in the sauce fixings and the broccoli.
3. Drain the noodles. Once the pan's hot, add the noodles and cover.
4. Simmer for a few minutes, occasionally stirring the noodles. Add a few tablespoons of water as needed.
5. Once the noodles have softened, mix everything until the ingredients are well distributed.
6. Extinguish the heat and leave the noodles in the pan until all the liquid in the bottom has been absorbed before serving.

Marinara Zoodles

Serving Portions: 4
Total Prep Time: 35 minutes
Macro Nutrients Each Serving:

- Carbs (net): 5.1 grams
- Calorie Amount: 179
- Protein Counts: 7 grams
- Fat Content (total): 18.8 grams

Essential Ingredients:

- Olive oil - ex. virgin (2 tbsp.)
- Garlic cloves (6)
- White onions (.5 cup)
- Tomatoes (14 oz./400 g - diced)
- Tomato paste (2 tbsp.)
- Basil leaves (.5 cup - loosely packed)
- Cayenne (1 pinch)
- Black pepper (.25 tsp.)
- Coarse salt (1.5 tsp.)
- Zucchinis (2 large spiralized)

Preparation Steps:

1. Warm the oil in a skillet on the stovetop using a medium-temperature setting.
2. Dice/mince and add the onion to the pan to sauté for about five minutes.
3. Mince and add the garlic. Cook approximately 60 seconds.
4. Roughly chop the basil. Mix in the salt, crushed red pepper flakes, pepper, salt, basil, tomato paste, and tomatoes. Combine thoroughly.
5. Simmer the sauce and lower the temperature setting to medium-low. Simmer until the oil takes on a deep orange color, indicating the sauce is thickened and reduced (15 min.). Season as desired.
6. Add in the zoodles and let them soften approximately two minutes before serving.

Mushroom & Cauliflower Risotto

Serving Portions: 4
Total Prep Time: 15 minutes
Macro Nutrients Each Serving:
- Carbs (net): 4.3 grams
- Calorie Amount: 186
- Protein Counts: 6 grams
- Fat Content (total): 17 grams

Essential Ingredients:
- Grated head of cauliflower (1)
- Vegetable stock (1 cup)
- Chopped mushrooms (9 oz./260 g)
- Butter (2 tbsp.)
- Coconut cream (1 cup)
- Pepper and salt (to taste)

Preparation Steps:
1. Pour the stock into a saucepan. Boil and set aside.
2. Prepare a skillet with butter and sauté the mushrooms until golden.
3. Grate and stir in the cauliflower and stock.
4. Simmer and add the cream, cooking until the cauliflower is al dente. Serve.

Mushroom Pasta With Shirataki Noodles

Serving Portions: 2
Total Prep Time: 20-25 minutes
Macro Nutrients Each Serving:
- Carbs (net): 4 grams
- Calorie Amount:
- Protein Counts: 6 grams
- Fat Content (total): 20 grams

Essential Ingredients:
- Shirataki noodles (2 packs @ 3 oz./85 g each)
- Butter (2 tbsp.)
- Garlic (2 cloves)
- Assorted mushrooms (3 cups)
- Almond flour (1 tsp.)
- Dried parsley (1 pinch)
- Thick cream (3/4 of 1 tub)
- Salt (.25 tsp.)
- Pepper (.25 tsp.)
- Olive oil
- *The Garnish*: Freshly chopped parsley

Preparation Steps:
1. Toss the shirataki noodles into a dry frying pan using the medium heat temperature setting. Continue to cook until you hear a whistling sound, indicating the excess moisture leaving the noodles. Transfer to the countertop to cool.
2. Toss the butter into the skillet with the garlic. Sauté it for approximately one minute or until it is fragrant.
3. Pour in the oil and add the mushrooms. Sauté for another five minutes, occasionally stirring until the mushrooms are golden in color. Transfer the mushrooms from the pan, leaving the oil behind.
4. Add the almond flour, salt, pepper, dried parsley, and cream. Stir and simmer to combine.
5. Lastly, toss the mushrooms and shirataki noodles into the skillet and combine. Serve right away.

Ramen Noodles

Serving Portions: 1
Total Prep Time: 45-50 minutes
Macro Nutrients Each Serving:
- Carbs (net): 7 grams
- Calorie Amount: 283
- Protein Counts: 16.5 grams
- Fat Content (total): 19 grams

Essential Ingredients:
Noodles & Broth:
- Sesame or olive oil (1 tbsp.)
- Tamari or coconut aminos (2 tbsp.)
- Veggie stock or bouillon and water (2 cups)
- Garlic clove (1 minced)
- Grated ginger (.125 tsp.)
- Shirataki noodles (1 pkg.)

The Toppings:
- Baked or fried tofu (¼ of a block)
- Baby spinach & Brussels sprouts (1 handful each)
- Mixed mushrooms (.25 cup)

To Garnish:
- Seaweed flakes
- Sesame seeds
- Chili flakes
- Chopped scallion

Preparation Steps:
1. Gather the ingredients. Sauté the mushrooms and bake the tofu, as needed. (Cube the tofu and marinate it in tamari. Bake for 30 minutes.)
2. Pour the oil into a saucepan using med-low heat. Toss in the garlic, ginger, and aminos/tamari. Sauté for a few minutes until everything smells delicious.
3. Drain and rinse noodles. Mix into the broth, and simmer for five to ten minutes.
4. Transfer the noodles from the broth using a spaghetti spoon or fork and place them at the

bottom of the bowl. Add the chosen toppings over the noodles.
5. Carefully pour broth over the toppings. Garnish with your choice of extra toppings.

Red Pepper Zoodles

Serving Portions: 4
Total Prep Time: 45-40 minutes
Macro Nutrients Each Serving:
- Carbs (net): 4.1 grams
- Calorie Amount: 198
- Protein Counts: 5 grams
- Fat Content (total): 16.7 grams

Essential Ingredients:
- Garlic (1 clove)
- Red bell peppers (1)
- Almond milk (1 cup)
- Olive oil (1 tbsp.)
- Almond butter (.25 cup)
- Salt (1 tsp.)

Preparation Steps:
1. Prepare a baking sheet by lining it with foil.
2. Add the bell peppers to the baking sheet before placing them on the top level of your broiler - letting them cook until blackened. Remove and cool.
3. Once they have cooled, you can remove the skins, stems, seeds, and ribs.
4. Add the prepared mixture, along with the remaining sauce ingredients, and blend thoroughly. Season as desired.
5. Serve with zoodles as well as a variety of potential toppings, including things like truffle oil, goat cheese, or parsley.

Zucchini Lasagna With Tofu Ricotta & Walnut Sauce

Serving Portions: 4
Total Prep Time: 45 minutes
Macro Nutrients Each Serving:
- Carbs (net): 10 grams
- Calorie Amount: 356
- Protein Counts: 17 grams
- Fat Content (total): 25 grams

Essential Ingredients:
The Sauce:
- Walnuts - finely ground (1 cup)
- Marinara sauce (divided - 1 jar/25 oz./710 g)
- Chopped sun-dried tomatoes (.25 cup)

The Lasagna:
- Zucchini (2)
- Tofu ricotta (1 batch)
- Optional: Nutritional yeast (2 tbsp.)

The Ricotta:
- Minced garlic (1 clove)
- Firm tofu (14 oz./400 g - firm - drained & pressed)
- Olive oil (1 tbsp.)
- Nutritional yeast (3 tbsp.)
- Dried basil (1 tbsp.)
- Lemon juice (1 tbsp.)
- Pepper and salt (to your liking)
- *Also Needed*: 7.5 by 9.5/19x24-cm baking pan

Preparation Steps:
1. Warm the oven in advance to reach 375° Fahrenheit/191° Celsius.
2. Slice the zucchini with a mandoline (11-inches lengthwise).
3. Prepare the ricotta by pulsing each of the fixings in a food processor until creamy smooth. Next, combine the marinara, walnuts, and sun-dried tomatoes - reserving ¾ cup for the pan.

4. Prepare the baking pan and add the reserved sauce with a layer of zucchini. Next, spread the tofu ricotta over the noodles, followed by a sprinkle of yeast. Finally, pour about half the walnut sauce over the top.
5. Layer until finished. Bake for 35 minutes or until done.

Zucchini Noodle Pasta With Avocado Pesto

Serving Portions: 8
Total Prep Time: 15-20 minutes
Macro Nutrients Each Serving:
- Carbs (net): 5.2 grams
- Calorie Amount: 214
- Protein Counts: 4.8 grams
- Fat Content (total): 17.1 grams

Essential Ingredients:
- Zucchinis (6 spiralized)
- Cold-pressed oil of choice (1 tbsp.)

The Pesto:
- Pine nuts (.25 cup)
- Avocados (2 cubed)
- Parsley leaves (.25 cup)
- Basil leaves (1 cup)
- Garlic (3 cloves)
- Lemon juice (1 lemon)
- Cold-pressed oil of choice (3 tbsp.)
- Salt and pepper (to your liking)

Preparation Steps:
1. Use a spiralizer to prepare the zucchini. Put the slices in a dish - cover them using a layer of paper towels to absorb the liquids.
2. Load your food processor with all of the pesto fixings (omit the oil). Pulse on low until desired consistency is reached.
3. Slowly add in olive oil until creamy and emulsified.
4. Heat one tablespoon of oil to your zucchini noodles pot and cook for 4 min.
5. Take your zucchini noodles and coat them with avocado pesto.

Sauces & Condiments

Avocado Mayonnaise

Serving Portions: 4
Total Prep Time: 6-8 minutes
Macro Nutrients Each Serving:
- Carbs (net): 1 gram
- Protein Counts: 1 gram
- Fat Content (total): 5 grams

Essential Ingredients:
- Ground cayenne pepper (.5 tsp.)
- Pinch of pink salt (1 pinch)
- Lime for juice (half of 1)
- Medium avocado (half of 1)
- Olive oil (.25 cup)
- Also Needed: Blender or food processor

Preparation Steps:
1. Dice the avocado. Combine the salt, cayenne, cilantro, avocado, and lime juice in the blender.
2. When smooth, stir in the oil (1 tbsp. at a time), pulsing in between each addition.
3. It stores in the refrigerator for up to one week in a sealed glass bottle.

Creamy Lemon Rosemary Salad Dressing

Serving Portions: 4
Total Prep Time: 5 minutes
Macro Nutrients Each Serving:
- Carbs (net): 1.7 grams
- Calorie Amount: 106
- Protein Counts: 1.5 grams
- Fat Content (total): 10.5 grams

Essential Ingredients:
- Fresh lemon juice (2 tbsp.)
- Garlic (1 small clove)
- White or red onion (2 tbsp.)
- Olive oil - ex. virgin (2 tbsp.)
- Sesame paste – tahini (2 tbsp.)
- Gluten-free Dijon mustard (.5 tsp.)
- Black pepper & sea salt (as desired)

Preparation Steps:
1. Mince the garlic. Chop the onion and squeeze the juice from the lemon.
2. Add all of the ingredients (omit the rosemary leaves) into a high-speed blender until smooth.
3. Add the rosemary and gently pulse enough to mix.
4. Keep the dressing in the refrigerator until it's time to serve.

Marinara Sauce

Serving Portions: 15
Total Prep Time: 15-18 minutes
Macro Nutrients Each Serving:
- Carbs (net): -0- grams
- Calorie Amount: 38
- Protein Counts: 1 gram
- Fat Content (total): 2 grams

Essential Ingredients:
- Olive oil (2 tbsp.)
- Garlic (1 clove)
- Onion flakes (2 tsp.)
- Finely chopped fresh thyme & Oregano (2 tsp. each)
- Tomato puree (24 oz. or 680 g)
- Vinegar - red wine (1 tbsp.)
- Erythritol - granulated (2 tsp.)
- Freshly cracked black pepper & salt (1 tsp. each)
- Fresh parsley (2 tbsp.)

Preparation Steps:
1. Use a saucepan to warm the oil. Mince and add the onion flakes, garlic, thyme, and oregano. Sauté them using the medium temperature setting (3 min.).
2. Pour in and mix the tomato puree, pepper, salt, erythritol, and red wine vinegar. Let it simmer.
3. Extinguish the heat. Finely chop and mix the parsley into the sauce and let it cool.
4. Pour it into a holding container in the refrigerator to use when needed.

Middle Eastern Tahini Sauce

Serving Portions: 1 cup
Total Prep Time: 10 minutes
Macro Nutrients Each Serving:
- Carbs (net): 3.1 grams
- Calorie Amount: 89
- Protein Counts: 2.8 grams
- Fat Content (total): 7.2 grams

Essential Ingredients:
- Tahini paste - liquids & solids (.5 cup)
- Warm tap water (.25 to .33 cup or as needed)
- Lemon juice (1-2 tbsp./more to taste)
- Optional: Olive oil (1-2 tbsp.)
- Garlic cloves (2)
- Kosher salt (.5 tsp.)
- Black pepper (.25 tsp.)

Spices to Garnish: As desired:
- Basil/mint
- Freshly chopped chives
- Italian parsley
- Your favorites

Preparation Steps:
1. If the tahini paste has separated, stir it while it's still in the jar with a fork before measuring. If the paste is chilled, wait for it to become room temp so that you can use both the solids and the oil.
2. Place tahini paste and warm water in a two-cup mason jar or medium mixing container - whisk until smooth. Once you start whisking, it will thicken, adding more water if using the mixture as a dressing.
3. Finely mince the garlic using a garlic press. Add the rest of the fixings into the jar – garlic, lemon juice, salt, pepper, and whisk until creamy and smooth. It will thicken as it cools in the refrigerator.
4. Taste and adjust the lemon and salt as desired.

Sugar-Free Sweet Soy Sauce

Serving Portions: 16
Total Prep Time: 25 minutes
Macro Nutrients Each Serving:
- Calorie Amount: 8
- Protein Counts: 2 grams
- Fat Content (total): -0- grams

Essential Ingredients:
- Tamari sauce (8 oz./230 g)
- Xylitol (1.25 cups)

Preparation Steps:
1. Toss the fixings into a saucepan using the low-temperature setting.
2. Warm the mixture until the xylitol has dissolved and the sauce has thickened slightly (15-20 min.).

Pour it into a holding container in the fridge for freshness.

Chapter 4: Lunch & Dinner Soup Options

Broccoli Soup With Curry

Serving Portions: 4
Total Prep Time: 35-40 minutes
Macro Nutrients Each Serving:
- Carbs (net): 4.8 grams
- Calorie Amount: 375
- Protein Counts: 16.9 grams
- Fat Content (total): 19.8 grams

Essential Ingredients:
- Salt & black pepper (as needed)
- Onion (1 chopped)
- Curry (1 tbsp.)
- Coconut oil (2 tbsp.)
- Vegetable stock (1 liter or 1.1 quarts)
- Coconut cream (1 cup)
- Cheese substitute - your choice (2.6 oz. or 75 g - grated)
- Broccoli (1 lb. or 450 g)

Preparation Steps:
1. Add oil into a skillet on the stovetop over a burner turned to the medium-high heat setting.
2. Mix in the onion. Simmer for approximately six minutes.
3. Lower the temperature to medium. Then, add in the broth until it begins to simmer. Mix in the broccoli and any seasonings before adding in the curry and letting it simmer for 20 minutes.
4. Pour into a blender before mixing in the cheese substitute.
5. Blend well.

Cauliflower-Tofu Curry Soup

Serving Portions: 1
Total Prep Time: 45 minutes
Macro Nutrients Each Serving:
- Carbs (net): 6 grams
- Calorie Amount: 638
- Protein Counts: 11 grams
- Fat Content (total): 65 grams

Essential Ingredients:
- Chopped cauliflower (.25 cup)
- Cumin (.5 tsp.)
- Paprika (.5 tsp.)
- Curry powder (.5 tsp.)
- Garlic powder (.5 tsp.)
- Olive oil (1.5 tbsp.)
- Butter (1.5 tbsp.)
- Heavy cream (.5 cup)
- Diced soft tofu (.5 cup)

Preparation Steps:
1. Heat the oven in advance to 425° Fahrenheit/218° Celsius.
2. Combine the chopped cauliflower with olive oil, garlic powder, curry powder, cumin, and paprika.
3. Arrange on a large baking tin and bake (20 min.).
4. Set aside to cool. When ready, pulse in a food processor until it has a rice-like texture and set it aside for now.
5. Pour the cream with the butter in a big saucepan and add the 'rice.'
6. Simmer for approximately five minutes and fold in the tofu. Stir and simmer for ten more minutes.
7. Spoon it into a serving dish to serve.

Egg Drop Soup

Serving Portions: 6
Total Prep Time: 25 minutes
Macro Nutrients Each Serving:
- Carbs (net): 2.9 grams
- Calorie Amount: 255
- Protein Counts: 10.8 grams
- Fat Content (total): 22.4 grams

Essential Ingredients:
- Vegetable broth (2 quarts/1.9 L.)
- Freshly chopped ginger (1 tbsp.)
- Turmeric (1 tbsp.)
- Sliced chili pepper (1 small)
- Coconut aminos (2 tbsp.)
- Minced garlic cloves (2)
- Large eggs (4)
- Mushrooms (2 cups sliced)
- Chopped spinach (4 cups)
- Sliced spring onions (2 medium)
- Freshly chopped cilantro (2 tbsp.)
- Black pepper (to your liking)
- Pink Himalayan (1 tsp.)
- For serving: Olive oil (6 tbsp.)

Preparation Steps:
1. Prep the Fixings: Grate the ginger root and turmeric. Mince the garlic cloves and slice the peppers and mushrooms.
2. Chop the chard stalks and leaves. Separate the stalks from the leaves. Dump the vegetable stock into a soup pot and simmer until it begins to boil. Toss in the garlic, ginger, turmeric, chard stalks, mushrooms, coconut aminos, and chili peppers. Boil for approximately five minutes.
3. Fold in the chard leaves and simmer for one minute.

4. Whip the eggs in a dish and add them slowly to the soup mixture. Stir until the egg is done and set it on the counter.
5. Slice the onions and chop the cilantro. Toss them into the pot.
6. Pour into serving bowls and drizzle with some olive oil (1 tbsp. per serving).
7. Serve warm or chilled.

Greens Soup

Serving Portions: 6
Total Prep Time: 10 minutes
Macro Nutrients Each Serving:
- Carbs (net): 5.7 grams
- Calorie Amount: 191
- Protein Counts: 6.3 grams
- Fat Content (total): 8.4 grams

Essential Ingredients:
- Spinach leaves (2 cups)
- Diced avocado (1)
- Diced English cucumber (.5 cup)
- Gluten-free vegetable broth (.25 cup)
- Black pepper and salt (as desired)

Preparation Steps:
1. Combine each of the fixings in the blender.
2. Toss in the fresh herbs and serve.

Minty Avocado Chilled Soup

Serving Portions: 2
Total Prep Time: 12-15 minutes
Macro Nutrients Each Serving:
- Carbs (net): 4 grams
- Calorie Amount: 280
- Protein Counts: 4 grams
- Total Fat Content: 26 grams

Essential Ingredients:
- Romaine lettuce (2 leaves)
- Ripened avocado (1 medium)
- Coconut milk (1 cup)
- Lime juice (1 tbsp.)
- Fresh mint (20 leaves)
- Salt (to your liking)

Preparation Steps:
1. Combine all of the fixings into a blender and mix well. You want it thick but not puree-like.
2. Chill it in the fridge for five to ten minutes before serving.

Pomodoro Soup

Serving Portions: 8
Total Prep Time: 25 minutes
Macro Nutrients Each Serving:
- Carbs (net): 6.5 grams
- Calorie Amount: 300
- Protein Counts: 11 grams
- Fat Content (total): 18 grams

Essential Ingredients:
- Coconut cream (1 cup)
- Veggie broth (29 oz./820 g)
- Tomatoes (3 lb./1.4 kg.)
- Diced onion (1)
- Vegan butter or your choice (3 tbsp.)

Preparation Steps:
1. Heat the Instant Pot using the sauté function. Once it's hot, add the butter to melt and toss in the onions to sauté (3-5 min.).
2. Stir in the tomatoes and simmer (2 min.).
3. Securely close the lid and set the soup function for six minutes.
4. Press the cancel button and wait about four to five minutes before you quick-release the pressure. Next, stir in the coconut cream - sauté for one minute.
5. Use a hand blender to puree the soup and serve.

Chapter 5: Veggies & Other Meals

Veggies

Broccoli & Cheese Casserole

Serving Portions: 5
Total Prep Time: 25-30 minutes
Macro Nutrients Each Serving:
- Carbs (net): 2 grams
- Calorie Amount: 113
- Protein Counts: 6 grams
- Fat Content (total): 9 grams

Essential Ingredients:
- Broccoli florets (2 cups)
- Onion (1 tbsp.)
- Fresh eggs (4)
- Mozzarella (.5 cup)
- Black pepper (.5 tsp.)
- Butter (2 tbsp.)

Preparation Steps:
1. Set the oven temperature to 350° Fahrenheit/177° Celsius.
2. Grease a baking dish and set it aside.
3. Melt the butter in a saucepan. Chop and add the onion and sauté until it's translucent.
4. Whisk the eggs and mix in with the onion. Sprinkle them with pepper and salt.
5. Toss in the florets in the prepared container and add the egg fixings.
6. Sprinkle with the cheese and bake until set or for about 13 minutes.
7. Set aside on a cooling rack to cool for two to three minutes before serving.

Broccoli Cauliflower Rice

Serving Portions: 4
Total Prep Time: 6-8 minutes
Macro Nutrients Each Serving:
- Carbs (net): 2 grams
- Calorie Amount: 91
- Protein Counts: 3 grams
- Fat Content (total): 8 grams

Essential Ingredients:
- Grated cauliflower (.5 lb./230 g)
- Broccoli - small pieces (4 oz./110 g)
- Water (2 tbsp.)
- Garlic salt (.25 tsp.)
- Butter (2 tbsp.)
- Cheese substitute - see recipes - your choice (2 tbsp.)
- Lemon zest (2 tsp.)
- Minced garlic (1 clove)
- Minced onion (3 oz./85 g)

Preparation Steps:
1. Chop the broccoli and grate the cauliflower - toss them into a microwavable container with the water. Prepare with a layer of plastic wrap on top using the high setting for two minutes.
2. Mince the garlic and onion.
3. Combine with the rest of the fixings and serve.

Buttered Brussels Sprouts

Serving Portions: 4
Total Prep Time: 30-35 minutes
Macro Nutrients Each Serving:
- Carbs (net): 6.8 grams
- Calorie Amount: 179
- Protein Counts: 4.2 grams
- Fat Content (total): 14.1 grams

Essential Ingredients:
- Fresh lemon juice (2 tbsp.)
- Salt (.5 tsp.)
- Ghee – melted (.25 cup)
- Brussels sprouts (1.1 lb./500 g)
- Pinch freshly ground black pepper

Optional Fixings:
- Garlic cloves (2 crushed)
- Sliced white onion (1 medium)
- Toasted pine nuts/flaked almonds/cashews (.25 cup)

Preparation Steps:
1. Prepare the oven in advance to reach 400° Fahrenheit/204° Celsius.
2. Rinse and quarter the sprouts and add the melted ghee along with a drizzle of the lemon juice. Add any other ingredients you like (calculate the calories, etc.).
3. Bake for 25-35 minutes until the outsides are crunchy. Stir occasionally.

Carrots & Sweet Potatoes

Serving Portions: 4
Total Prep Time: 20 minutes
Macro Nutrients Each Serving:
- Carbs (net): 6 grams
- Calorie Amount: 413
- Protein Counts: 7 grams
- Fat Content (total): 8 grams

Essential Ingredients:
- Sweet potatoes (2 lb./910 g)
- Olive oil (2 tbsp.)
- Chopped onion (1)
- Baby carrots (2 lb.)
- Vegetable broth (1 cup)

Preparation Steps:
1. Heat the Instant Pot using the sauté mode.
2. Cube the potatoes, slice the carrots into halves, and chop the onion.
3. Pour in the oil and add the onion to sauté them until softened (5 min.).
4. Stir in the rest of the fixings and close the top.
5. Use the manual setting on high for eight minutes.
6. Quick-release the built-up pressure and serve.

Cauliflower Spinach Bowl

Serving Portions: 1
Total Prep Time: 30 minutes
Macro Nutrients Each Serving:
- Carbs (net): 7 grams
- Calorie Amount: 499
- Protein Counts: 17 grams
- Fat Content (total): 44.6 grams

Essential Ingredients:
- Cauliflower (.75 cups)
- Spinach (1 cup)
- Almonds (.25 cup)
- Garlic (.25 tbsp.)
- Cilantro (.5 cup)
- Sunflower seeds (.5 tbsp.)
- Olive oil (2 tbsp.)
- Ricotta cheese (.5 tbsp.)

Preparation Steps:
1. Chop the cauliflower, garlic, and onions.
2. Heat the oven to reach 375° Fahrenheit/191° Celsius.
3. Add the almonds to a baking tin to roast them for seven to ten minutes. Set the pan to the side for a few minutes to cool.
4. Use a food processor and add the cauliflower. Pulse until it's rice-like.
5. In another skillet, heat one tablespoon of oil using the medium heat setting. Toss in the riced cauliflower and chopped garlic - sauté them until golden brown and sprinkle with pepper and salt.
6. Mix in the cilantro and spinach, but don't stir - let them wilt on top for two to three minutes.
7. Garnish with the sunflower seeds, almonds, and ricotta before serving.

Creamy Spinach-Rich Ballet

Serving Portions: 4
Total Prep Time: 35-40 minutes
Macro Nutrients Each Serving:
- Carbs (net): 2.9 grams
- Calorie Amount: 188
- Protein Counts: 14.6 grams
- Fat Content (total): 12.5 grams

Essential Ingredients:
- Fresh baby spinach (1.5 lb./680 g)
- Coconut cream (8 tsp.)
- Sliced cauliflower (14 oz./400 g)
- Melted - unsalted butter (2 tbsp.)
- Black pepper and salt (as desired)
- Also Needed: 4 ramekins

Preparation Steps:
1. Heat the oven to reach 360° Fahrenheit/182° Celsius.
2. Prepare a skillet with butter. Toss in the spinach to saute for three minutes.
3. Drain the juices from the spinach and add to the ramekins.
4. Slice the cauliflower and add to the containers with cream, salt, and pepper.
5. Bake for 25 minutes and serve warm.

Creamy-Style Green Cabbage

Serving Portions: 4
Total Prep Time: 10-15 minutes
Macro Nutrients Each Serving:
- Carbs (net): 8.2 grams
- Calorie Amount: 432
- Protein Counts: 4.2 grams
- Fat Content (total): 42.3 grams

Essential Ingredients:
- Butter (2 oz./56 g)
- Shredded green cabbage (1.5 lb./680 g)
- Coconut cream (1.25 cups)
- Finely chopped fresh parsley (8 tbsp.)
- Pepper & Salt (to your liking)

Preparation Steps:
1. Shred the cabbage and add to a skillet with the butter to sauté till they're a nice golden brown.
2. Stir in the cream with a sprinkle of pepper and salt - simmer.
3. Garnish with the parsley and serve while warm.

Easy Roasted Veggies - Sheet Pan

Serving Portions: 8
Total Prep Time: 30-35 minutes
Macro Nutrients Each Serving:
- Carbs (net): grams
- Calorie Amount: 97
- Protein Counts: 7 grams
- Fat Content (total): 11 grams

Essential Ingredients:
- Pepper (.25 tsp.)
- Red onion (1)
- Balsamic vinegar (1 tbsp.)
- Coarse salt (1 tsp.)
- Red bell peppers (2)
- Italian seasoning (2 tsp.)
- Butternut squash (3 cups)
- Olive oil - ex. virgin (3 tbsp.)
- Broccoli florets (4 cups)

Preparation Steps:
1. Heat the oven to 425° Fahrenheit/218° Celsius.
2. Cube and toss the squash in a" T" of oil and spread out onto a baking tray. Roast for about ten minutes.
3. Chop the onion and red peppers. Cube the squash and cut the broccoli into florets.
4. Toss with the salt, pepper, Italian seasoning, bell peppers, onion, and broccoli until well coated.
5. Add the roasted squash to the veggies. Toss well and spread the veggie mixture over two baking trays.
6. Roast them, stirring one or two times during the cooking process. The veggies should be tender and browned (17-20 min.).
7. Drizzle with vinegar before eating.
8. These would be great for meal prep since they will stay fresh in the fridge for up to a week.

Eggplant Hash - Moroccan Style

Serving Portions: 8
Total Prep Time: 10-15 minutes
Macro Nutrients Each Serving:
- Carbs (net): 5.3 grams
- Calorie Amount: 798
- Protein Counts: 9.4 grams
- Fat Content (total): 55.8 grams

Essential Ingredients:
- Coconut oil olive or ghee (2 tbsp.)
- Eggplant - salted (1 large)
- Red bell peppers (2 small)
- Red onion (1 medium)
- Garlic cloves (4)
- Slivered almonds toasted (.25 cup)
- Sun-dried tomatoes in oil (.5 cup)
- Fresh mint leaves - whole (.25 cup)
- Cinnamon ground (.5 tsp.)
- Coriander seed ground (.5 tsp.)
- Cayenne pepper powder (.25 tsp.)
- Salt & black pepper (as desired)

Preparation Steps:
1. Heat a big pan or wok using a high-temperature setting.
2. Drain the oil from the tomatoes and dice.
3. Dice/mince the onion and garlic.
4. Remove the pepper seeds. Cube and salt the eggplant and peppers.
5. Pour in the oil and swirl it to coat the pan. Toss in the peppers and eggplant with a sprinkle of salt and pepper. Sear for about one minute.
6. Add your onions and garlic, then toss the ingredients together and allow them to simmer for about two more minutes.

7. Add sun-dried tomatoes, almonds, and fresh mint leaves. Dust your ingredients with your spices, toss to mix everything, and serve.

Lemon Green Beans with Almonds

Serving Portions: 4
Total Prep Time: 15 minutes
Macro Nutrients Each Serving:
- Carbs (net): 6.5 grams
- Calorie Amount: 131
- Protein Counts: 3.5 grams
- Fat Content (total): 9.8 grams

Essential Ingredients:
- Garlic (4 cloves)
- Fresh green beans (1 lb. or 450 g)
- Unrefined sea salt (.5 tsp.)
- Sliced organic almonds (.33 or 1/3 cup)
- Lemon juice (1-2 tbsp. - fresh)
- Olive - ex. virgin (2 tbsp.)

Preparation Steps:
1. Trim the beans and steam until tender and crispy. Add the salt and lemon juice - toss gently. Squeeze fresh lemons for juice.
2. Warm the olive oil in a pan using the med-lo setting. Blend in the almonds and cook until the almonds start changing colors and add the garlic. Continue cooking for 30 seconds. Cook the garlic for no more than 60 seconds because it will lose its nutrients.
3. Mix everything and toss well.

Mexican Cauli-Rice

Serving Portions: 4
Total Prep Time: 15-20 minutes
Macro Nutrients Each Serving:
- Carbs (net): 5.4 grams
- Calorie Amount: 121
- Protein Counts: 3.5 grams
- Fat Content (total): 7.6 grams

Essential Ingredients:
- White onion (half of 1 medium)
- Clove of garlic (1)
- Olive oil - ex. virgin (2 tbsp.)
- Cumin (1 tsp.)
- Chili powder (1 tbsp.)
- Cauliflower (1 lb. riced)
- Diced tomatoes – no salt (1 can - 14.5 oz./410 g) Pink Himalayan salt/sea salt (as desired)
- *Possible Garnishes:*
- Sliced avocado
- Limes
- Minced cilantro
- Sliced jalapeno
- Sour cream
- Extra-virgin olive oil

Preparation Steps:
1. Use the medium temperature setting on the stovetop and pour in the oil. Dice/mince and toss in the onions and garlic and to sauté for two to three minutes. When they are soft, add the spices and continue sauteing for 30 seconds or so.
2. Toss in the riced cauliflower and sauté for another five to seven minutes until it starts to get crispy around the edges. It will look similar to fluffed rice.
3. Add salt if you wish and serve.

Mushrooms & Broccoli

Serving Portions: 4
Total Prep Time: 25 minutes
Macro Nutrients Each Serving:
- Carbs (net): 2.3 grams
- Calorie Amount: 81
- Protein Counts: 2.1 grams
- Fat Content (total): 7 grams

Essential Ingredients:
- Sliced mushrooms (1 cup)
- Broccoli florets (2 cups)
- Coconut oil (1 tbsp.)
- Veggie broth (1 cup)
- Liquid aminos/Soy sauce sub. (1 tbsp.)

Preparation Steps:
1. Choose the sauté mode and add the coconut oil to the Instant Pot to melt.
2. When it's hot, toss in the mushrooms to sauté (4-5 min.).
3. Stir in the soy sauce and broccoli. Continue cooking for one more minute.
4. Empty in the broth and secure the lid of the cooker.
5. Use the high setting and set the timer for two minutes.
6. Quick-release the pressure when done.
7. Serve the veggies with a spritz of the cooking juices.

Pesto Roasted Cabbage & Mushrooms

Serving Portions: 1
Total Prep Time: 30 minutes
Macro Nutrients Each Serving:
- Carbs (net): 8 grams
- Calorie Amount: 576
- Protein Counts: 13 grams
- Fat Content (total): 55.6 grams

Essential Ingredients:
- Cabbage (.75 cup)
- Pesto sauce (2 tbsp.)
- Hard cheese - Italian style - grated (.2 tbsp.)
- Feta cheese (.25 cup - crumbled)
- Fresh basil (1 tbsp.)
- White mushrooms (.25 cup)
- Olive oil (2 tbsp.)

Preparation Steps:
1. Set the oven in advance to 375° Fahrenheit/191° Celsius.
2. Shred the cabbage - chop the mushrooms and basil.
3. Arrange the mushrooms and cabbage on a baking tray.
4. Spritz with the oil and toss evenly.
5. Scoop some pesto sauce on top and toss again. Add the grated cheese over the top and bake for about 20 minutes.
6. Serve with a portion of crumbled feta and basil.

Rutabaga Cakes

Serving Portions: 12
Total Prep Time: 35-40 minutes
Macro Nutrients Each Serving:
- Carbs (net): 2.1 grams
- Calorie Amount: 46
- Protein Counts: 0.4 grams
- Fat Content (total): 3.9 grams

Essential Ingredients:
- Melted butter (half of 1 stick)
- Rutabagas (2)
- Fresh thyme (2 tbsp.)
- Salt (2 tsp.)
- Also Needed: Muffin tin

Preparation Steps:
1. Set the oven to reach 350° Fahrenheit/177° Celsius.
2. Chop the thyme.
3. Prepare a saucepan with the butter and toss in the thyme. Sauté it for about two minutes.
4. Thinly slice the rutabaga into a dish and add the butter mixture over them.
5. Layer them in the muffin tin. Spritz it using the remainder of the butter.
6. Set a timer to bake for 25 to 30 minutes.

Stuffed Mushrooms

Serving Portions: 4
Total Prep Time: 25-30 minutes
Macro Nutrients Each Serving:
- Carbs (net): 2.6 grams
- Calorie Amount: 124
- Protein Counts: 5 grams
- Fat Content (total): 22.4 grams

Essential Ingredients:
- Portobello mushrooms (4)
- Blue cheese (1 cup)
- Olive oil (2 tbsp.)
- Fresh thyme (1 pinch)
- Salt (as desired)

Preparation Steps:
1. Heat the oven to reach 350° Fahrenheit/177° Celsius.
2. Cut the stems from the mushrooms and chop them to bits.
3. Mix with the thyme, salt, and crumbled blue cheese, and stuff the mushrooms.
4. Spritz with some of the oil.
5. Bake for 15-20 minutes. Serve piping hot.

Whole Roasted Cauliflower with Tahini Sauce

Serving Portions: 4
Total Prep Time: 1 hour 40 minutes
Macro Nutrients Each Serving:
- Carbs (net): 3 grams
- Calorie Amount: 127
- Protein Counts: 5 grams
- Fat Content (total): 8 grams

Essential Ingredients:
- Cauliflower (1 whole - large)
- Olive oil - divided (2 tbsp.)
- Salt (.5 tsp.)
- Optional: Zaatar/dukkah spice (1 tbsp.) **
- Water (1 cup)

Tahini sauce (1 batch - chapter 3)

Possible Garnishes:
- Chili flakes
- Dill
- Mint
- Drizzle of sauce

Preparation Steps:
1. Preheat the oven to reach 425° Fahrenheit or 218° Celsius.
2. Trim the cauliflower. It is easier to remove the stem. However, you can also leave it as one piece by slicing the bottom to stand straight.
3. Toss them into a Dutch oven or another ovenproof skillet.
4. Drizzle oil (1 tbsp.) over the cauliflower - dusting it using salt and Zaatar spice. Pour water (1 cup) into the bottom of the pan.
5. Cover the pan with foil or a lid to bake until tender in the middle when pierced with a knife (45 min. to 1 hr.).

6. Make the tahini sauce. Carefully remove the lid/foil when ready.
7. Drizzle with a tiny bit of oil, pop it into the oven for ½ hour, rotating halfway through.
8. Transfer the pan from the oven once it is nicely browned.
9. Garnish it to your liking and serve.
10. Note: ** You can also mix cumin, coriander, or sumac.

Other Favorites

Zucchini-Tomato Gratin

Serving Portions: 6

Total Prep Time: 50-55 minutes

Macro Nutrients Each Serving:
- Carbs (net): 2.5 grams
- Calorie Amount: 114
- Protein Counts: 7 grams
- Fat Content (total): 8 grams

Essential Ingredients:
- Garlic powder (1 tsp.)
- Basil (2 tsp.)
- Salt (.5 tsp.)
- Onion (.5 cup)
- Garlic (2 tbsp.)
- Olive oil (2 tbsp.)
- Tomatoes (2)
- Zucchini (3)

Preparation Steps:
1. Set the oven setting at 350° Fahrenheit/177° Celsius.
2. Chop and sauté the onions until they are fragrant and translucent.
3. Mince and toss in the garlic, sautéing for one to two minutes longer. Pour the mixture into the bottom of a casserole dish.
4. Slice the tomatoes and zucchinis.
5. Layer the zucchini and tomatoes, alternating layers.
6. Spritz the veggies using a bit of olive oil. Then, dust it with seasonings and cover with your keto-friendly cheese of choice.
7. Bake until the gratin turns a light brown (40 min.).
8. Serve it when it is ready.

Asian Garlic Tofu

Serving Portions: 4
Total Prep Time: 1.5 hours - varies
Macro Nutrients Each Serving:
- Carbs (net): 14 grams
- Calorie Amount: 467
- Protein Counts: 45.9 grams
- Fat Content (total): 28.5 grams

Essential Ingredients:
- Hoisin sauce (.25 cup)
- Sesame oil (1 tsp.)
- Super-firm tofu (1 pkg.)
- Red pepper flakes (.25 tsp.)
- Ginger garlic paste (1 tsp.)
- For the Garnish: Chopped green onions

Preparation Steps:
1. Wrap the tofu with paper towels and place a heavy skillet on top for about half of an hour.
2. Combine the rest of the fixings and set them aside.
3. Slice the tofu into cubes and place in the marinade for about 40 minutes.
4. Warm the oil in the skillet and add the tofu.
5. Sauté it until done on all sides and serve warm with a portion of green onions.

Asparagus & Tofu Mash

Serving Portions: 1
Total Prep Time: 15-20 minutes
Macro Nutrients Each Serving:
- Carbs (net): 8 grams
- Calorie Amount: 601
- Protein Counts: 20 grams
- Fat Content (total): 57.3 grams

Essential Ingredients:
- Coconut oil (2 tbsp.)
- Asparagus (.5 cup)
- Spring onions (1 tbsp.)
- Silky tofu (1 cup)
- Coconut cream (4 tbsp.)
- Parsley (.5 tbsp.)
- Lemon juice (1 tsp.)

Preparation Steps:
1. Chop the spring onion, asparagus, and tofu.
2. Prepare the cubed tofu in a steamer unit for eight to ten minutes.
3. Fill a pot of water and wait for it to boil. Toss in the asparagus for about two minutes to blanch and drain.
4. Use medium heat on the stovetop and add the oil to sauté the onions.
5. Toss all of the fixings into a blender and mix until creamy smooth.

Serve piping hot.

Black Bean Quiche

Serving Portions: 6
Total Prep Time: 50-55 minutes
Macro Nutrients Each Serving:
- Carbs (net): 5.1 grams
- Calorie Amount: 141.7
- Protein Counts: 10 grams
- Fat Content (total): 8.7 grams

Essential Ingredients:
- Eggs (5 whole & 5 whites)
- Water (.33 cup)
- Salt (.5 tsp.)
- Black pepper (.25 tsp.)
- Chopped tomato (.5 cup)
- Low-sodium black beans (.66 or 2/3 cup)
- Jack cheese - grated (3 oz./85 g)
- To Garnish: Cilantro

Preparation Steps:
1. Whisk all of the eggs with salt, pepper, and water.
2. Set the oven to 375° Fahrenheit/191° Celsius.
3. Empty the mixture into a greased pie dish coated with a spritz of cooking oil spray.
4. Sprinkle with the beans, tomatoes, and cheese.
5. Bake for 30 to 35 minutes until the centers of the eggs are set.
6. Let them cool for about ten minutes and sprinkle with the cilantro before serving.

Broccoli & Tofu Stir Fry

Serving Portions: 1
Total Prep Time: 50-55 minutes
Macro Nutrients Each Serving:
- Carbs (net): 4 grams
- Calorie Amount: 433
- Protein Counts: 23 grams
- Fat Content (total): 50 grams

Essential Ingredients:
- Firm tofu (.5 cup)
- Broccoli (.5 cup)
- Sesame seeds (1 tsp.)
- Olive oil (1.5 tbsp.)
- Soy sauce (.5 tbsp.)
- Chili powder (.5 tsp.)
- Sesame oil (1 tbsp.)
- Slivered almonds (1 tbsp.)

Preparation Steps:
1. Cube the tofu and chop the broccoli.
2. Set the oven temperature to 425° Fahrenheit/218° Celsius.
3. Prepare a baking pan using oil (½ tbsp.), pepper, and salt. Toss in the tofu and bake until the outside is crunchy (25-30 min.).
4. Combine the sesame oil and the rest of the olive oil in a big skillet using a high-temperature setting,
5. Toss in the almonds to sauté for about one to two minutes. Fold in the tofu.
6. Stir in the broccoli and continue cooking for another four to five minutes until the broccoli is a bright green.
7. Stir and add the keto-friendly soy sauce. Simmer one more minute and serve with a garnish of sesame seeds.

Buddha Bowl - Vegan-Friendly

Serving Portions: 1
Total Prep Time: 40 minutes
Macro Nutrients Each Serving:
- Carbs (net): 13 grams
- Calorie Amount: 641
- Protein Counts: 23 grams
- Fat Content (total): 50 grams

Essential Ingredients:
- Broccoli florets (1.5 cups)
- Brussels sprouts (1 cup)
- Tahini (2 tbsp.)
- Oil (.5 tsp.)
- Pumpkin seeds (2 tbsp.)
- Salt (1 pinch)
- Kalamata olives (10)
- For the Topping: Avocado & sesame seeds

Preparation Steps:
1. Heat the oven to reach 425° Fahrenheit/218° Celsius.
2. Cover a baking tray using a layer of aluminum foil. Add the pumpkin seeds, brussels sprouts, and broccoli.
3. Toss well with tahini, salt, and oil. Bake for about 35 minutes.
4. Remove the tray from the oven and toss with the olives.
5. Serve with the sliced avocado with a sprinkle of the delicious sesame seeds.

Burritos - Vegan-Friendly - Instant Pot

Serving Portions: 8
Total Prep Time: 40-45 minutes
Macro Nutrients Each Serving:
- Carbs (net): 11 grams
- Calorie Amount: 475
- Protein Counts: 9 grams
- Fat Content (total): 38 grams

Essential Ingredients:
The Filling:
- Water or olive oil for sautéing (2-3 tbsp.)
- Cloves of garlic (3)
- Medium red onion (1)
- Red bell pepper - diced (1 small)
- Black beans (15 oz. can)
- Uncooked short grain brown rice (1.5 cups)
- Corn – fresh – canned - frozen (1.5 cups)
- Finely chopped kale (1 cup)
- Salsa (12 oz./340 g)
- Water (2 cups)
- Ground cumin (1 tsp.)
- Chili powder (2 tsp.)
- Salt (1 tsp. more as desired)
- Smoked paprika (1 tsp.)

For Serving:
- 10-12-inch Burrito flour tortillas (8)
- Chopped lettuce (2-3 cups)
- Avocados (1-2 chopped or sliced)

Optional:
- Green or red onion - chopped
- More salsa
- Chopped tomatoes
- Jalapenos
- Vegan sour cream or vegan cheese shreds

Preparation Steps:
1. Choose the sauté mode on the Instant Pot.

2. Pour in the oil or water. Dice and toss in the garlic, onion, and red pepper. Stir while cooking (2-3 min.). Add more water as needed. Turn off the sauté function.
3. Drain and rinse the beans. Combine each of the remaining burrito filling ingredients into the Instant Pot. Stir well, secure the lid, turn the valve to seal, and set to the high-pressure setting (24 min.).
4. Natural-release the pressure for about 3 minutes, and quick-release the rest. Carefully remove the top to stir the mixture. Taste and add more spices or salt if desired.
5. Spoon some of the prepared burrito mixture onto the centers of the flour tortillas.
6. Add the desired amount of lettuce, avocado, and other fixings.
7. Fold the two sides over the filling and roll them to serve.

Celery Fries & Tempeh

Serving Portions: 6
Total Prep Time: 1 hour 10 minutes
Macro Nutrients Each Serving:
- Carbs (net): 3.5 grams
- Calorie Amount: 278
- Protein Counts: 19 grams
- Fat Content (total): 28.7 grams

Essential Ingredients:
The Chicken:
- Salt & Pepper (as desired)
- Olive oil (2 tbsp.)
- Tempeh (24 oz./680 g - divided)

The Fries:
- Salt (.5 tsp.)
- Pepper (.25 tsp.)
- Root celery (1.5 lb./680 g)
- Olive oil (2 tbsp.)

Preparation Steps:
1. Warm the oven - set at 400° Fahrenheit/204° Celsius.
2. Set your grill to a high-temperature setting.
3. Cube the tempeh before placing it in a saucepan - covering it in water.
4. Put the pan on the stove using the high-temperature setting.
5. Once the water boils, lower the temperature setting - simmer for about ten minutes.
6. Drain the water and place the tempeh in a large mixing container before adding in two tablespoons of olive oil and seasoning as needed. Allow the tempeh to marinate for at least 15 minutes.
7. Meanwhile, cut the root celery into strips and place it in a mixing bowl before adding in the remaining olive oil and seasoning as needed. Shake well to coat.
8. Arrange the celery strips on a baking tin to bake (20 min.).

135

9. Grill the tempeh for about five minutes per side. Serve when ready.

Eggplant Burgers - Instant Pot

Serving Portions: 4
Total Prep Time: 20 minutes
Macro Nutrients Each Serving:
- Carbs: 20 grams
- Calorie Amount: 170
- Protein Counts: 15 grams
- Fat Content (total): 36 grams

Essential Ingredients:
- Water (1 cup)
- Large eggplant (1)
- Panko breadcrumbs (.5 cup)
- Olive oil (2 tbsp.)
- Mustard (2 tbsp.)

Preparation Steps:
1. Add the water to the Instant Pot.
2. Rinse and trim the eggplant and slice it into four rounds. Arrange in the cooker and secure the top. Set the timer for two minutes using the high-pressure setting.
3. When it's done, quick-release the built-up pressure and drain the eggplant, discarding the liquid.
4. Brush them with mustard and a coating of panko.
5. Add the oil to the pot and arrange the burgers to cook using the sauté mode.
6. Serve with or without a bun.

Falafel With Tahini Sauce

Serving Portions: 4 @ 2 per serving
Total Prep Time: 25-30 minutes
Macro Nutrients Each Serving:
- Carbs (net): 5 grams
- Calorie Amount: 281
- Protein Counts: 8 grams
- Fat Content (total): 24 grams

Essential Ingredients:
- Raw pureed cauliflower (1 medium head - 1 cup - florets only)
- Ground cumin (1 tbsp.)
- Ground slivered almonds (.5 cup)
- Cayenne pepper (.5 tsp.)
- Ground coriander (.5 tbsp.)
- Kosher salt (1 tsp.)
- Eggs (2 large)
- Freshly chopped parsley (2 tbsp.)
- Garlic clove (1 minced)
- Coconut flour (3 tbsp.)

The Sauce:
- Water (4 tbsp.)
- Tahini paste (2 tbsp.)
- Salt (1 tsp.)
- Minced garlic clove (1)
- For Cooking: Grapeseed or olive oil
- Lemon juice (1 tbsp.)

Preparation Steps:
1. Puree enough cauliflower to make one cup with a grainy texture. Process the almonds the same way, but _don't over-grind._
2. Combine the first group of fixings in a mixing container until thoroughly blended.
3. Warm half of the mixture of olive and grape seed oil. Make (8) 3-inch patties and add to the pan.

4. Use the rest of the oil if needed. Cook until browned and flip. Continue cooking for about four minutes. Add them to a platter for the oil to drain.
5. Mix all of the tahini fixings in a bowl, adding water a little at a time until it reaches the texture desired.
6. Serve when ready.

Ginger Sesame Walnut & Hemp Seed Lettuce Wraps

Serving Portions: 4
Total Prep Time: 1 hour 15 minutes
Macro Nutrients Each Serving:
- Carbs (net): 10 grams
- Calorie Amount: 382
- Protein Counts: 14 grams
- Fat Content (total): 31 grams

Essential Ingredients:
The Sauce:
- Low-sodium tamari (2 tbsp.)
- Brown rice vinegar (2 tbsp.)
- Minced ginger (1 tbsp.)
- Pure maple syrup (1 tbsp.)
- Toasted sesame oil (1 tsp.)

The Filling:
- Hemp seeds (.5 cup)
- Walnuts (1 cup)
- Dates (2)
- Cucumber (.5 cup)
- Carrots (.25 cup)
- Lettuce leaves
- Optional: Sesame seed

Preparation Steps:
1. Combine all of the sauce fixings.
2. Chop the dates, walnuts, carrots, and cucumbers.
3. Combine the sauce with the rest of the filling fixings. Put it in the refrigerator to chill for one hour.
4. Remove and pile onto the leaves of lettuce and top off with the seeds as desired.

Mixed Veggie Patties - Instant Pot

Serving Portions: 4
Total Prep Time: 15-20 minutes
Macro Nutrients Each Serving:
- Carbs (net): 3 grams
- Calorie Amount: 220
- Protein Counts: 4 grams
- Fat Content (total): 10 grams

Essential Ingredients:
- Cauliflower florets (1 cup)
- Frozen vegetables (1 bag - mixed)
- Water (1.5 cups)
- Flax meal (1 cup)
- Olive oil (2 tbsp.)

Preparation Steps:
1. Fill the Instant Pot with the water and add the veggies to the steamer basket. Secure the lid and set the timer for four to five minutes using the high-pressure setting.
2. Quick-release the pressure and drain.
3. Use a potato masher and stir in the flax meal. Shape into four patties.
4. Select the sauté mode using a clean pot - pour in the oil.
5. Prepare the patties until they are golden brown or for about three minutes on each side before serving.

Mini Shepherd's Pie- Instant Pot - Vegan-Friendly

Serving Portions: 3
Total Prep Time: 30-35 minutes
Macro Nutrients Each Serving:
- Carbs (net): 4.7 grams
- Calorie Amount: 225
- Protein Counts: 12 grams
- Fat Content (total): 14 grams

Essential Ingredients:
- Water (1.5 cups)
- Cauliflower (2 cups)
- Diced onion (1 cup)
- Grated potatoes (1 cup)
- Diced tomatoes (1 cup)

Preparation Steps:
1. Steam and mash the cauliflower.
2. Set the Instant Pot using the sauté mode - adding a splash of water. Toss in the onions. Cook slowly for two minutes. Grate the potatoes and add to the mix and sauté for five more minutes. Pour in the tomatoes and continue sauteing for three additional minutes.
3. Prepare each of the ramekins with a spritz of cooking oil spray. Portion the fixings and top it off with the mashed potatoes.
4. Add the water and the trivet into the cooker and secure the lid.
5. Set the timer for five minutes on the high setting.
6. Serve when the time is up - after a ten-minute natural release of the pressure.

Mushroom & Spinach Pie

Serving Portions: 6
Total Prep Time: 1.5 hours - varies
Macro Nutrients Each Serving:
- Carbs (net): 5.6 grams
- Calorie Amount: 266
- Protein Counts: 19.3 grams
- Fat Content (total): 17.5 grams

Essential Ingredients:
- Garlic (1 tsp.)
- Mushrooms (8 oz. or 230 g)
- Fresh spinach (10 oz. or 280 g)
- Oil (2 tsp.)
- Grated cheese of choice - keto-friendly (2 tbsp.)
- Eggs (4)
- Cottage cheese (16 oz./450 g)
- Heavy cream (.5 cup)
- Pepper (.5 tsp.)
- Salt (1 tsp.)
- Nutmeg (.25 tsp.)
- Shredded cheese for the topping (.5 cup)

Preparation Steps:
1. Lightly grease a baking dish.
2. Set the oven temperature setting at 350° Fahrenheit/177° Celsius.
3. Thinly slice the mushrooms and dice the garlic.
4. Warm the oil in a skillet and sauté the mushrooms and garlic until tender. Fold in the spinach with nutmeg, pepper, and salt. Simmer till the spinach wilts.
5. Drain the fixings in a colander.
6. Sprinkle the cheese (2 tbsp.) on the pie plate.
7. Whisk the cottage cheese with the eggs and cream. Finally, stir in the mushroom mixture.
8. Pour the mixture into the pan with the last of the shredded cheese (.5 cup).

9. Bake for 50 to 60 minutes. Watch closely; turn down if it's cooking too fast. Turn off the oven and let it sit for about ten minutes before serving.

Pumpkin-Cheddar Risotto

Serving Portions: 3
Total Prep Time: 25 minutes
Macro Nutrients Each Serving:
- Carbs (net): 3.1 grams
- Calorie Amount: 223
- Protein Counts: 9.4 grams
- Fat Content (total): 16.3 grams

Essential Ingredients:
- Riced cauliflower (12 oz./340 g)
- Onion (half of 1 medium)
- Butter (2 tbsp.)
- Paprika (2 tsp.)
- Pumpkin puree (.5 cup)
- Shredded sharp cheddar cheese - keto-friendly (3 oz./85 g)
- Pepper & salt (as desired)

Preparation Steps:
1. Prepare a saucepan with butter. Dice and sauté the onion with paprika, pepper, and salt until it's softened.
2. Combine the puree and the cauliflower - last.
3. Place a top on the pan and simmer for about 15 minutes. Stir occasionally - until it's softened.
4. Remove and combine with the cheese of choice.

Radish & Zucchini Quiche

Serving Portions: 4
Total Prep Time: 55 minutes to 1 hour
Macro Nutrients Each Serving:
- Carbs (net): 5 grams
- Calorie Amount: 248
- Protein Counts: 13.3 grams
- Fat Content (total): 19.4 grams

Essential Ingredients:
- Zucchini (1)
- Eggs (8)
- Thinly sliced garlic cloves (2)
- Coconut cream (.5 cup)
- Fresh herbs (1 bunch - ex. rosemary, thyme, tarragon, etc.)
- Sea salt (4.5 tsp.)
- Cubed radishes (.5 lb. or 230 g)
- Ground black pepper (.5 tsp.)
- Coconut oil - frying - as needed

Preparation Steps:
1. Set the oven temperature to reach 325° Fahrenheit/163° Celsius.
2. Heat the oil in the skillet. Chop and toss in the zucchini and garlic to sauté for five minutes.
3. Whisk the eggs, salt, and coconut cream together.
4. Lightly grease a pie dish with a spritz of cooking oil spray. Cube the radishes. Arrange the zucchini and radish in the dish and add the egg mixture.
5. Bake until the top is starting to brown to serve (45 min.).

Sloppy Joes - Vegan-Friendly

Serving Portions: 6
Total Prep Time: 55-60 minutes
Macro Nutrients Each Serving:
- Carbs (net): 8.9 grams
- Calorie Amount: 354
- Protein Counts: 14.7 grams
- Fat Content (total): 29.9 grams

Essential Ingredients:
- Hulled hemp seeds (.5 cup)
- Hulled pumpkin seeds - Pepitas (1 cup)
- Chopped walnuts (1 cup)
- Apple cider vinegar (1 tbsp.)
- Vegetable broth (2 cups)
- Tomato paste (6 oz./170 g)
- Prepared mustard (1 tbsp.)
- Garlic powder (.5 tbsp.)
- Granulated sweetener (1 tbsp.)
- Onion powder (1 tsp.)
- Lettuce wraps - for serving

Preparation Steps:
1. Combine each of the fixings in a soup pot using a med-low temperature setting.
2. Place the top on the pot. Simmer gently for about 45 minutes, occasionally stirring until the vegetable broth is completely absorbed.
3. Serve on keto rolls or bread.

Spicy Tofu & Eggplant

Serving Portions: 1
Total Prep Time: 45-50 minutes
Macro Nutrients Each Serving:
- Carbs (net): 5 grams
- Calorie Amount: 512
- Protein Counts: 21 grams
- Fat Content (total): 58.6 grams

Essential Ingredients:
- Firm tofu cubes (.5 cup)
- Green snap beans (1 tbsp.)
- Diced eggplant (.25 cup)
- Chopped garlic (.5 tsp.)
- Keto-friendly soy sauce (.5 tbsp.)
- Olive oil (2 tbsp.)
- Cider vinegar (.25 tbsp.)
- Sesame oil (1.5 tbsp.)
- Chopped red chili (1 tbsp.)

Preparation Steps:
1. Set the oven temperature to reach 425° Fahrenheit/218° Celsius.
2. Mix the tofu with pepper, salt, and oil (½ tbsp.). Toss.
3. Arrange the prepared tofu on a baking tray (tofu not touching).
4. Bake until the edges are firm or for 25-30 minutes.
5. Pour in the remainder of the olive oil and sesame oil into a large skillet using the high-temperature setting. Toss in the garlic and eggplant. Simmer for five to six minutes until softened.
6. Fold in the tofu and stir. Next, fold in the green beans, red chili, vinegar, and soy sauce of choice. Simmer for about two to three more minutes.
7. Serve hot.

Spicy Tofu Taco

Serving Portions: 1
Total Prep Time: 40-45 minutes
Macro Nutrients Each Serving:
- Carbs (net): 6 grams
- Calorie Amount: 614
- Protein Counts: 17 grams
- Fat Content (total): 59 grams

Essential Ingredients:
- Egg (1)
- Coconut flour (.5 cup)
- Avocado oil (1 tbsp.)
- Lime juice (1 tbsp.)
- Shredded romaine lettuce (1 cup)
- Chopped red onion (1 tbsp.)
- Firm tofu (.5 cup)
- Olive oil (2 tbsp.)
- Paprika (.25 tbsp.
- Sliced avocado (.125 cup)

Preparation Steps:

1. Preheat the oven to reach 350° Fahrenheit/177° Celsius.
2. Prepare a baking pan with a sheet of parchment paper.
3. Cube the tofu and toss into the oil and paprika. Sprinkle it using pepper and salt as desired.
4. Arrange the tofu in the pan and bake for 25-30 minutes until it's crispy and firm. Transfer to the counter and set aside.
5. Make the tortillas by combining avocado oil, coconut flour, and egg. Whisk well.
6. Warm a small pan and spritz with a bit of avocado oil.
7. Add a spoonful of the mixture in the pan for a diameter of six to eight inches. Once firm, flip it over for another two to three seconds.
8. Continue with the batter until done.
9. Mix the avocado slices, lettuce, and onion. Toss and work the tofu with a drizzle of lime juice.
10. Add three tablespoons of the filling to each of the tortillas and serve.

Spinach Quiche Without a Crust

Serving Portions: 1
Total Prep Time: 35-40 minutes
Macro Nutrients Each Serving:

- Carbs (net): 7 grams
- Calorie Amount: 567
- Protein Counts: 30 grams
- Fat Content (total): 47 grams

Essential Ingredients:

- Spinach (1 cup)
- Egg (1)
- Shredded cheddar (.5 cup)
- Crumbled blue cheese (.25 cup)
- White chopped onion (1 tbsp.)
- Chopped garlic (.5 tbsp.)
- Milk - your choice (.25 cup)
- Butter (1 tbsp.)

Preparation Steps:

1. Heat the oven to reach 375° Fahrenheit/191° Celsius.
2. Lightly grease a round baking dish with butter.
3. Combine the spinach, egg, onion, cheddar, blue cheese, milk, and garlic. Mix well.
4. Pour into the pan and bake until the edges are browned (approximately 30 minutes or so). Remove and cool before serving.

Thai-Inspired Peanut Red Curry Bowl

Serving Portions: 1
Total Prep Time: 15-20 minutes
Macro Nutrients Each Serving:
- Carbs (net): 10.4 grams
- Calorie Amount: 355
- Protein Counts: 15.8 grams
- Fat Content (total): 23.4 grams

Essential Ingredients:
- Sesame oil (1 tsp.)
- Shirataki noodles (8 oz./230 g pkg.)
- Peanut butter - unsweetened (2 tbsp.)
- Tamari - l. s. (2 tsp.)
- Thai red curry paste (2-3 tsp.)
- Grated ginger (.25 tsp.)
- Fresh edamame (.25 cup)
- Fresh lime juice (1 tsp.)

Suggested Optional Fixings:
- Red pepper flakes (1 pinch)
- Chopped peanuts
- Additional lime juice

Preparation Steps:
1. Thoroughly rinse and drain the noodles and add to a frying pan using a medium-low temperature setting. Cook for a few minutes until the noodles are mostly dry.
2. Stir in the curry paste, tamari, peanut butter, sesame oil, grated ginger, and bell peppers. Stir until a sauce forms, and everything is evenly coated.
3. Simmer for about three to five more minutes or until the peppers soften, and everything is thoroughly heated.
4. Transfer the hot curry to a bowl and top with edamame and other desired toppings.

Tomato-Cheese Frittata

Serving Portions: 4
Total Prep Time: 10 minutes
Macro Nutrients Each Serving:
- Carbs (net): 7.4 grams
- Calorie Amount: 435
- Protein Counts: 26.7 grams
- Fat Content (total): 32.6 grams

Essential Ingredients:
- Eggs (6)
- Soft cheese - feta (ex. 3.5 oz. or 2/3 cup)
- White onion (half of 1 medium or 1.9 oz.)
- Halved cherry tomatoes (2/3 cup)
- Chopped herbs - ex. basil or chives (2 tbsp.)
- Ghee/butter (1 tbsp.)

Preparation Steps:
1. Program the oven broiler to reach 400° Fahrenheit/204° Celsius.
2. Dice and add onions into a greased, hot iron skillet and cook with ghee/butter until slightly brown.
3. In a separate dish, crack the eggs, add salt, pepper, or add herbs if you wish. Whisk and add to the onion pan.
4. Cook until the edges begin to brown. Top with the cheese and tomatoes.
5. Put the pan in the broiler for five to seven minutes or until done.

Zucchini Lasagna With Tofu Ricotta & Walnut Sauce

Serving Portions: 4
Total Prep Time: 55-60 minutes
Macro Nutrients Each Serving:
- Carbs (net): 10 grams
- Calorie Amount: 356
- Protein Counts: 17 grams
- Fat Content (total): 25 grams

Essential Ingredients:

The Sauce:
- Walnuts - finely ground (1 cup)
- Marinara sauce (divided - 1 jar or 25 oz./710 g)
- Chopped sun-dried tomatoes (.25 cup)

The Lasagna:
- Zucchini (2)
- Tofu Ricotta (1 batch)
- Nutritional Yeast - optional (2 tbsp.)

The Ricotta:
- Lemon juice (1 tbsp.)
- Minced garlic (1 clove)
- Firm tofu (14 oz./400 g - firm drained & pressed)
- Olive oil (1 tbsp.)
- Pepper & salt (as desired)
- Dried basil (1 tbsp.)
- Nutritional yeast (3 tbsp.)
- Suggested Baking Pan: 7.5 x 9.5-inches

Preparation Steps:
1. Warm the oven to reach 375° Fahrenheit/191° Celsius.
2. Slice the zucchini with a mandoline (11-inches lengthwise).
3. Prepare the ricotta by pulsing all of the fixings in a food processor until creamy.
4. Combine the marinara and walnuts with the sun-dried tomatoes - reserving ¾ cup for the pan.

5. Prepare the baking tray and add the reserved sauce with a layer of zucchini. Spread the tofu ricotta over the noodles, followed by a sprinkle of the yeast. Pour about half the walnut sauce on the top.

Layer until finished and bake for 35 minutes until done.

Chapter 6: Vegetarian Snack Options

Avocado-Cucumber Gazpacho

Serving Portions: 6
Total Prep Time: 5-6 minutes
Macro Nutrients Each Serving:
- Carbs (net): 5.7 grams
- Calorie Amount: 131
- Protein Counts: 2.3 grams
- Fat Content (total): 10.4 grams

Essential Ingredients:
- Medium cucumbers (2)
- Chopped avocados (1.5)
- Basil leaves (.33 or 1/3 cup - loosely packed)
- Water (1 to 1.5 cups)
- Black pepper & salt (as desired)

Preparation Steps:
1. Peel, remove the seeds - chop the cucumbers and avocados.
2. Toss everything into a blender. Mix well and adjust with pepper and salt.
3. Serve.

Cauliflower Hummus

Serving Portions: 2 cups
Total Prep Time: 50 minutes
Macro Nutrients Each Serving:
- Carbs (net): 1 gram
- Calorie Amount: 1 tbsp. each - 41 cal.
- Protein Counts: 1 gram
- Fat Content (total): 4 grams

Essential Ingredients:
- Cauliflower (1 small head/440 g)
- Garlic (1 clove/3 g)
- Tahini (.33 cup (163 gm))
- Lemon juice - fresh (1 tbsp./15 g)
- Avocado oil (.25 cup/56 g)
- Sea salt (1 pinch)

Preparation Steps:
1. Chop the cauliflower into small chunks. Toss them in with olive oil.
2. Arrange the diced cauliflower in a roasting pan and bake at 375° Fahrenheit or 191° Celsius (40 min.). Gently toss them about halfway through the baking cycle. Cool for a few minutes.
3. Combine the prepared cauliflower with the remainder of the fixings in a blender and mix until it's creamy smooth.
4. When done, pour it into a closed container and use it for up to seven days.

Chocolate & Hazelnut Spread

Serving Portions: 6
Total Prep Time: 10-15 minutes
Macro Nutrients Each Serving:
- Carbs (net): 2 grams
- Calorie Amount: 271
- Protein Counts: 4 grams
- Fat Content (total): 28 grams

Essential Ingredients:
- Unsalted butter (1 oz./28 g)
- Coconut oil (.25 cup)
- Hazelnuts (5 oz./140 g)
- Cocoa powder (2 tbsp.)
- Optional: Erythritol (1 tsp.)
- Vanilla extract (1 tsp.)

Preparation Steps:
1. Prepare a skillet on the stovetop until hot. Toss in the hazelnuts and roast until golden. Let them cool slightly.
2. Arrange the nuts in a kitchen towel to rub away some of the shells. (If they're stuck, that is okay.)
3. Toss all of the fixings into a blender/processor. Mix well to reach the desired consistency.
4. *Special Treat*: Serve as a delicious and healthy dip for fresh strawberries or as a spread for rolls, waffles, or pancakes.

Classic Guacamole

Serving Portions: 4 @ .25 cup each
Total Prep Time: 15 minutes
Macro Nutrients Each Serving:
- Carbs (net): 1.5 grams
- Calorie Amount: 101
- Protein Counts: 1 gram
- Fat Content (total): 10 grams

Essential Ingredients:
- Hass Avocado - mashed (230 g/1 cup)
- Cilantro (.25 cup/4 g)
- Spring onion (10 g/1 tbsp.)
- Jalapeño pepper (14 g/medium)
- Lime juice (15 g/1 tbsp.)
- Garlic (2.8 g/1 tsp.)
- Avocado oil (15 g/1 tbsp.)
- Salt (as desired)

Preparation Steps:
1. Thinly slice the spring onion. Next, mince the garlic, jalapeno, and cilantro.
2. Toss each of the fixings into a mixing container to thoroughly mix.
3. Add a layer of plastic cling wrap over the guacamole, pressing to remove air, and add a lid to the container. Pop it into the refrigerator to chill.

Flaxseed Crackers

Serving Portions: 6
Total Prep Time: Varies - 18 hours
Macro Nutrients Each Serving:
- Carbs (net): 4.1 grams
- Calorie Amount: 123
- Protein Counts: 4 grams
- Fat Content (total): 14.6 grams

Essential Ingredients:
- Flax seeds (1 cup)
- Red pepper flakes (.5 tsp.- optional)
- Water (1 cup)
- Onion powder (.5 tsp. - optional)
- Rosemary (1 tsp. - optional)
- Garlic powder (.5 tsp. - optional)

Preparation Steps:
1. Dump the flax seeds into a bowl and put the dish into the fridge for up to 18 hours.
2. Take the seeds out and place them on a sheet of parchment paper. Roll as thin as you can get them.
3. Warm the oven to reach 275° Fahrenheit/135° Celsius and cook the seeds for an hour on the baking paper. Serve with your favorite dip.

Granola

Serving Portions: 12
Total Prep Time: 2.5 hours - varies
Macro Nutrients Each Serving:
- Carbs (net): 0.4 grams
- Calorie Amount: 337
- Protein Counts: 7.9 grams
- Fat Content (total): 31.6 grams

Essential Ingredients:
- Coconut oil (.3 cup)
- Swerve (.5 cup)
- Salt (1 tsp.)
- Raw walnuts (.5 cup)
- Raw almonds (.5 cup)
- Pumpkin seeds (1 cup)
- Vanilla extract (1 tsp.)
- Raw sunflower seeds (1 cup)
- Raw pecans (.5 cup)
- Raw hazelnuts (.5 cup)
- Cinnamon (1 tsp.)
- Stevia - vanilla flavor (1 tsp.)
- Unsweetened shredded coconut (1 cup)

Preparation Steps:
1. Warm the Instant Pot using the sauté function.
2. Then, add the coconut oil to melt. When melted, add the vanilla extract and stevia. Stir well before adding the coconut, seeds, and nuts. Finally, stir to coat all of the ingredients.
3. In a mixing container, whisk the cinnamon, salt, and swerve. Sprinkle with the seeds and nuts.
4. Close and seal the lid. Set on slow cook using the low setting for two hours and stir every 30 minutes.
5. When done, just quick-release the built-up steam pressure.
6. Spread onto a baking pan to cool.

Olive & Tomato Fat Bombs

Serving Portions: 5
Total Prep Time: 45 minutes + chill time
Macro Nutrients Each Serving:
- Carbs (net): 1.7 grams
- Calorie Amount: 164
- Protein Counts: 3.7 grams
- Fat Content (total): 17.1 grams

Essential Ingredients:
- Salt (.25 tsp.)
- Black pepper (as desired)
- Garlic (2 cloves crushed)
- Kalamata olives (4 pitted)
- Sun-dried tomatoes (4 pieces - drained)
- Thyme (2 tbsp.)
- Oregano (2 tbsp.)
- Basil (2 tbsp.)
- Coconut oil (.25 cup)
- Coconut cream (.5 cup)
- Cheese substitute - your choice (8 oz./230 g)

Preparation Steps:
1. Pour the coconut oil into a small mixing dish with the cream and leave them both to soften for about ½ hour. Mash - mixing well to combine.
2. Finely chop the oregano, thyme, and basil.
3. Drain the tomatoes. Add in the Kalamata olives and tomatoes and mix well before adding in the herbs and seasonings. Combine thoroughly before placing the mixing bowl in the refrigerator to allow the results to solidify.
4. Once it's solidified, form the mixture into a total of five balls using an ice cream scoop or similar spoon. Roll each of the finished balls in cheese substitute before plating.
5. Extras can be stored in the fridge for up to seven days.

Tortilla Chips/Nachos with Salsa

Serving Portions: 5
Total Prep Time: 6¾ hours
Macro Nutrients Each Serving:
- Carbs (net): 6 grams
- Calorie Amount: 411
- Protein Counts: 13.6 grams
- Fat Content (total): 35 grams

Essential Ingredients:
- Coconut flour (1.5 tbsp.)
- Flax meal/ground flaxseed (1/3 c. + 1 tbsp.)
- Almond flour (.5 cup)
- Whole psyllium husks (1 tbsp.)
- Ground chia seeds (1 tbsp.)
- Lukewarm water (.5 cup + 1-2 tbsp. more as needed if the dough is dry)
- Salt – pink Himalayan (.5 tsp.)
- E.V. olive oil/ghee for brushing (2 tbsp.)
  Ingredients for the Salsa
- Garlic (2 cloves)
- Tomatoes- unsweetened & peeled (14.1 oz./400 g)
- Red chili pepper (1 small)
- Ghee/extra-virgin coconut oil (2 tbsp.)
- Jalapeno peppers (2 - pickled or fresh)
- Dried oregano (2 tsp.)
- Pepper and salt (as desired)
  The Topping - Optional:
- Grated hard cheese – cheddar/Manchego/etc. (3.5 oz./99 g)

Preparation Steps:
1. Prepare the oven to 400°F before you begin.
2. Flatten the dough in between two sheets of parchment paper until thin. Then, use a sharp knife or pizza slicer to cut the triangles.
3. Brush each of the chips with ghee/oil and arrange them on a paper-lined baking sheet.

4. Bake for 10-15 minutes.
5. Make the salsa by peeling and finely dicing the chili peppers and garlic. Add to a greased skillet with two tablespoons of ghee using the medium heat setting until lightly browned.
6. Blend in the oregano, salt, pepper, and tomatoes along with the jalapenos. Stir well and simmer for ten minutes after lowering the temperature to low.
7. In the meantime, grate the cheese and set it aside.
8. You can serve as a dipping dish or scoop the chips into four bowls, add ¼ of the salsa, and garnish with the cheese or other goodies.

Zucchini Grilled Cheese Sandwich

Serving Portions: 2
Total Prep Time: 1¼ hours
Macro Nutrients Each Serving:
- Carbs (net): 6 grams
- Calorie Amount: 936
- Protein Counts: 29 grams
- Fat Content (total): 90.1 grams

Essential Ingredients:
- Shredded zucchini (2 cups)
- Egg (1)
- Shredded Italian-style hard cheese (.125 cup)
- Shredded cheddar cheese (.5 cup)
- Green sliced onions - sliced (.25 cup)
- Cornstarch (.25 tbsp.)
- Coconut oil (4 tbsp.)

Preparation Steps:
1. Shred the zucchini and wrap in towels for about one hour. Then, use a skillet or other heavy object over it to squeeze out the extra liquids.
2. Combine with the egg, cornstarch, cheese, and onions. Sprinkle it with pepper and salt. Toss well.
3. Pour the oil in a skillet to cover the pan and warm using a medium heat temperature setting. When it's hot, add about ¼ of the zucchini mixture into the skillet, shaping it into a square.
4. Simmer until golden and drain the grease using paper towels.
5. In the same pan, add two zucchini patties and top with the cheddar cheese - add the second patty on top to make a sandwich.

Chapter 7: Vegetarian Dessert Options

Chocolate Mousse

Serving Portions: 2
Total Prep Time: 10 minutes + chill time
Macro Nutrients Each Serving:
- Carbs (net): 4 grams
- Calorie Amount: 460
- Protein Counts: 4 grams
- Fat Content (total): 50 grams

Essential Ingredients:
- Butter (4 tbsp.)
- Cream cheese (4 tbsp.)
- Heavy whipping cream (1.5 tbsp.)
- Swerve or another natural sweetener (1 tbsp.)
- Unsweetened cocoa powder (1 tbsp.)

Preparation Steps:
1. Remove the butter and cream cheese from the fridge about ½ hour before time to prepare to become room temperature.
2. Chill a bowl and whisk the cream. Place back in the refrigerator for now.
3. Use a hand mixer to combine the sweetener, cream cheese, cocoa powder, and butter until well mixed.
4. Remove the refrigerated cream and fold it into the chocolate mixture using a rubber scraper.
5. Portion into two dessert bowls and chill for one hour.

Coconut Granola Bars

Serving Portion: 12
Total Prep Time: 3¼ hours
Macro Nutrients Each Serving:
- Carbs (net): 0.7 grams
- Calorie Amount: 102
- Protein Counts: 14.2 grams
- Fat Content (total): 12.7 grams

Essential Ingredients:
- Flaxseed eggs (2)
- Medjool dates (4 - chopped)
- Sea salt (.5 tsp.)
- Baking powder (.5 tsp.)
- Chia seeds (2 tbsp.)
- Ground vanilla beans (2 tsp.)
- Coconut (.25 cups - shredded)
- Flax meal (.25 cup)
- Coconut butter (.5 cup)
- Maple syrup (.5 cup)
- Rolled oats (1.5 cups - gluten-free)
- Also Needed: Slow cooker

Preparation Steps:
1. Add the oats, ground vanilla beans, flax meal, shredded coconut, and baking powder together in a small bowl and mix thoroughly.
2. In another container, mix the dates, maple syrup, and flax eggs.
3. Then, mix the two bowls of ingredients thoroughly.
4. Grease the slow cooker and line it with a sheet of parchment paper.
5. Add the ingredients to the cooker and pat it down well.
6. Adjust the slow cooker temperature to low and close the lid for about 2.5 hours. It's done when the middle ceases to be mushy.

7. After the bars have finished cooking, remove them by gently pulling out the parchment paper.
8. Cool them for 40 minutes before cutting them into bars.

Cream Crepes

Serving Portions: 4
Total Prep Time: 10 minutes
Macro Nutrients Each Serving:
- Carbs (net): 2.5 grams
- Calorie Amount: 145
- Protein Counts: 3.5 grams
- Fat Content (total): 13.1 grams

Essential Ingredients:
- Organic eggs (2)
- Coconut flour (2 tbsp.)
- Coconut cream (.33 cup)
- Melted - divided coconut oil (2 tbsp.)
- Splenda/your favorite keto sweetener (1 tsp.)

Preparation Steps:
1. Whisk the sweetener of choice with the eggs and oil until smooth.
2. Stir in the flour and cream; slowly - while blending well.
3. Pour about ¼ of the batter into a skillet and cook for approximately two minutes per side. Scoop a portion of whipped cream on top and serve.

Crunch-Berry Mousse

Serving Portions: 8
Total Prep Time: 4 hours to chill + 10-15 minutes
Macro Nutrients Each Serving:
- Carbs (net): 3 grams
- Calorie Amount: 260
- Protein Counts: 3 grams
- Fat Content (total): 27 grams

Essential Ingredients:
- Heavy whipping cream (2 cups)
- Vanilla extract (.25 tsp.)
- Lemon (half of 1 - zested)
- Chopped pecans (2 oz./56 g)
- Fresh raspberries/blueberries/strawberries (3 oz./85 g)

Preparation Steps:
1. Use a hand mixer to whip the cream until it forms soft peaks. Then, add the vanilla and lemon zest when formed.
2. Fold in the nuts and berries. Stir.
3. Cover with a layer of plastic wrap.
4. For a firmer mousse, store in the fridge for about four hours.
5. You can enjoy it when freshly prepared if you like it less firm.

Ginger Snap Cookies

Serving Portions: 1
Total Prep Time: 20 minutes
Macro Nutrients Each Serving:
- Carbs (net): 2.2 grams
- Calorie Amount: 74
- Protein Counts: 2.3 grams
- Fat Content (total): 6.7 grams

Essential Ingredients:
- Unsalted butter (.25 cup)
- Egg (1 large)
- Almond flour (2 cups)
- Ground cinnamon (.5 tsp.)
- Vanilla extract (1 tsp.)
- Sugar substitute/Erythritol/Swerve (1 cup)
- Ground ginger (2 tsp.)
- Ground cloves (.25 tsp.)
- Nutmeg (.25 tsp.)
- Salt (.25 tsp.)

Preparation Steps:
1. Prepare the oven temperature to reach 350° Fahrenheit/177° Celsius.
2. Whisk the dry components in a mixing bowl. Blend in the rest of the ingredients into the dry mixture using a hand blender.
   (The dough will become stiff.)
3. Measure out the dough for each cookie and flatten them using a fork or your fingers. Bake until browned (9-11 min.).

Lime Cheesecake Bites

Serving Portions: 10
Total Prep Time: 8-10 minutes + time to chill (2 hours)
Macro Nutrients Each Serving:
- Carbs (net): 5.6 grams
- Calorie Amount: 249
- Protein Counts: 5.1 grams
- Fat Content (total): 23.6 grams

Essential Ingredients:
   The Crust:
- Walnuts - or any nut seed (.33 cup)
- Almonds - or any nut seed (.5 cup)
- Unsweetened coconut shreds - or sub with any nut seed (.33 cup)
- Coconut oil (1 tbsp.)
- Lakanto powdered monkfruit (1 tsp.)
- dash of pink salt
- Water (1 tbsp.)
   The Filling:
- Raw cashews (.75 cup)
- Fresh spinach (1 cup/1 big handful)
- Unsweetened cashew/almond milk (.5 cup)
- Almond butter (3 tbsp.)
- Lakanto powdered monkfruit (2.5 tbsp.) or Homemade powdered monkfruit/coconut sugar (5 tbsp./as desired to taste)
- Lime zest - divided (1 tbsp./3 medium limes)
- Lime juice (3-4 tbsp.)
- Vanilla (1 tsp.)
- Pink salt (1 pinch)
- Coconut oil - melted (.33 cup)
- Suggested Loaf Pan Size: 7x3-inch/19x24-cm

Preparation Steps:
1. Cover a small loaf pan with parchment baking paper.
2. Pulse each of the fixings - except water - in a food processor/small blender until coarse crumbs form.

3. Pulse until crumbs stick together when pinched (adding water if needed).
4. Press one crust mixture into the pan. Pop the pan into the fridge and prepare the filling.
5. For the filling, reserve a sprinkle of zest - if desired. Then, toss all of the ingredients - except oil - into a small blender cup and blend till it's smooth.
6. Taste and adjust for sweetness. Add in the melted oil - blend again.
7. Dump the filling over the crust - optional - sprinkle with remaining zest, and freeze for one to two hours until firm throughout - then refrigerate till you're ready to serve.
8. Keep refrigerated for about five days or frozen for one month in an airtight container.

Mini Berry Blender Cheesecakes

Serving Portions: 18
Total Prep Time: 10 minutes + chilling time (1 hour)
Macro Nutrients Each Serving:
- Carbs (net): 3.1 grams
- Calorie Amount: 133
- Protein Counts: 3 grams
- Fat Content (total): 12 grams

Essential Ingredients:
- Nuts or almonds & coconut (1.33 cups)
- Coconut oil - melted (2 tbsp.)
- Water (2-3 tbsp.)
- Monkfruit - or coconut sugar (1 tbsp.)
- Pink salt (1 pinch)
- Vanilla (1 splash)
  The Filling:
- Raw cashews (1 cup)
- Chopped berries - half of each - blackberries & strawberries (1 cup)
- Coconut sugar or powdered monkfruit (.25 cup/to taste)
- Coconut oil - melted (.25 cup)
- Lemon juice - divided (1 tbsp. + 1 tsp.)
- Water (2 tbsp.)
- Pink salt (1 pinch)

Preparation Steps:
1. Cover a cupcake pan using a layer of parchment baking paper or foil wrappers. You can also use a mini cupcake pan lined using strips of parchment paper (½ by 4-inch strips) for easy removal.
2. Pulse each of the fixings (omit the water) in a small blender or food processor to create fine crumbs.
3. Add water as needed and pulse until crumbs stick together when pinched.

4. Press the crust mixture (1-2 tbsp.) firmly into each wrapper. Then, pop it into the fridge while you prepare the filling.
5. Toss the fruit, cashews, sweetener, juice of lemon, water, and salt into the blender cup and pulse until smooth.
6. Taste and adjust the filling for sweetness. Melt and add oil - pulse the mixture once more.
7. Divide the prepared filling into the chilled crusts. Freeze or chill until firm (1-2 hrs.).
8. Serve when it is ready as desired!

Mini Coconut Pies

Serving Portions: 12
Total Prep Time: 55 minutes
Macro Nutrients Each Serving:
- Carbs (net): 3 grams
- Calorie Amount: 174
- Protein Counts: 3 grams
- Fat Content (total): 13 grams

Essential Ingredients:
- Coconut oil (1 tbsp.)
- Coconut flour (1 cup)
- Large eggs (2)
- Melted ghee (.5 cup)
- Vanilla bean sweetener - sugar-free (3 tbsp.)
- Coconut cream - unsweetened (1 cup)
- Shredded coconut - unsweetened (.25 cup)
- Also Needed: 12-count mini muffin tray

Preparation Steps:
1. Set the oven to 350° Fahrenheit/177° Celsius.
2. Lightly grease the cups of the tray using coconut oil.
3. Whisk the eggs with ghee, coconut flour, and one tablespoon of the vanilla bean sweetener in a mixing container.
4. Portion the flour mixture between the mini-muffin cups and pat it into the bottom of each cup. Set a timer to bake for ten minutes.
5. Thoroughly cool - transfer the coconut pie shells from the baking tin.
6. Use a small mixing container to combine the shredded coconut with the coconut cream rest of the sweetener (2 tbsp.).
7. Top each pie shell with about one tablespoon of the cream mixture. Chill the pies for at least ½ hour before serving time.
8. Garnish them using a portion of toasted coconut as desired to serve.

Peanut Butter Fudge

Serving Portions: 20
Total Prep Time: 1 hour 10 minutes
Macro Nutrients Each Serving:
- Carbs (net): 6 grams
- Calorie Amount: 135
- Protein Counts: 4 grams
- Fat Content (total): 11 grams

Essential Ingredients:
- Coconut oil (3 tbsp.)
- Smooth peanut butter - keto-friendly (12 oz./340 g)
- Coconut cream (4 tbsp.)
- Maple syrup (4 tbsp.)
- Salt (1 pinch)

Preparation Steps:
1. Prepare a baking sheet with a layer of parchment paper.
2. Melt the syrup and coconut oil using a medium-temperature setting on the stovetop.
3. Mix in the salt, coconut cream, and peanut butter - adding it to the prepared tray. Then, pop it into the fridge to chill for at least one hour.
4. Slice into pieces and store or serve.

Pudding Pops

Serving Portions: 1
Total Prep Time: 10-15 minutes + chill time
Macro Nutrients Each Serving:
- Carbs (net): 1.2 grams
- Calorie Amount: 122
- Protein Counts: 2.8 grams
- Fat Content (total): 10.3 grams

Essential Ingredients:
- Gelatin (1 tsp.)
- Coconut or almond milk - from a carton (1 cup)
- Cocoa powder (2 tbsp.)
- Cream cheese (6 oz./170 g)
- Liquid stevia (20 drops)
- Erythritol powder (1 tbsp.)
- Vanilla extract (1 tsp.)

Preparation Steps:
1. Prepare a saucepan using a low-temperature setting. Add the milk. Mix in the gelatin slowly to dissolve. Remove from the burner when it starts steaming. Pour into a spouted container such as a measuring cup.
2. Combine the remainder of the fixings and use a blender to mix well.
3. Pour into a popsicle mold. Freeze for at least two hours.

Pumpkin Bars With Cream Cheese Frosting

Serving Portions: 16
Total Prep Time: 45 minutes
Macro Nutrients Each Serving:

- Carbs (net): 2 grams
- Calorie Amount: 139
- Protein Counts: 3 grams
- Fat Content (total): 13 grams

Essential Ingredients:

- Large eggs (2)
- Coconut oil (.25 cup)
- Cream cheese (2 oz.)
- Pumpkin puree (1 cup)
- Almond flour (1 cup)
- Vanilla extract (1 tsp.)
- Gluten-free baking powder (2 tsp.)
- Erythritol sweetener blend (.66 cups
- Pumpkin pie spice (1 tsp.)
- Sea salt (.5 tsp.)
  The Frosting:
- Powdered erythritol (.5 cup)
- Optional: Heavy cream (1 tbsp.)
- Softened cream cheese (6 oz.)
- Vanilla extract (1 tsp.)
- Also Needed: 9 x 9 baking pan

Preparation Steps:

1. Warm the oven until it reaches 350° Fahrenheit/177° Celsius.
2. Cover the baking pan with parchment paper.
3. In a double boiler or microwave, melt the coconut oil and cream cheese.
4. Combine the vanilla, eggs, cream cheese mixture, and puree using a hand mixer until smooth using the medium-speed setting.
5. Whisk the dry fixings (salt, pie spice, baking powder, sweetener, and flour).

6. Mix all the ingredients with the mixer until just combined and pour into the pan.
7. Bake for 20-30 minutes. Cool completely.
8. Prepare the frosting with each of the ingredients when the bars are cooled. If it's too thick, just add a little cream or milk.
9. Slice into 16 equal portions. Enjoy any time.

Delicious Fat Bombs

Blueberry Frozen Fat Bombs

Serving Portions: 24
Total Prep Time: 10 minutes + chilling time
Macro Nutrients Each Serving:
- Carbs (net): 1 gram
- Calorie Amount: 116
- Protein Counts: 0.44 grams
- Fat Content (total): 13 grams

Essential Ingredients:
- Blueberries (1 scant cup)
- Coconut oil (.75 cup)
- Butter (1 stick)
- Softened cream cheese (4 oz./110 g)
- Coconut cream (.25 cup)
- Sweetener of choice (to taste)

Preparation Steps:
1. Thoroughly rinse and arrange three to four berries in each mold cup.
2. Melt the butter with the coconut oil over the lowest stovetop heat setting. Cool slightly for approximately five minutes.
3. Combine all of the ingredients and whisk well. Then, slowly, add the sweetener.
4. Using a spouted pitcher, fill an ice tray with 24 bombs.
5. Pop them out to eat.

Chocolate-Cherry Fat Bombs

Serving Portions: 20 bars
Total Prep Time: 10 minutes
Macro Nutrients Each Serving:
- Carbs (net): 3 grams
- Calorie Amount: 200
- Protein Counts: 1 gram
- Fat Content (total): 16 grams

Essential Ingredients:
- Unsweetened shredded coconut (2.25 cups)
- Unsweetened dried cherries (.25 cup)
- Pure keto-friendly maple syrup - Lakanto brand (.25 cup)
- Coconut butter - melted (1 cup)
- Keto - sugar-free chocolate chips (2 cups)

Preparation Steps:
1. Add your unsweetened shredded coconut with dried cherries and blend until just mixed in a high-speed blender or food processor. Pour into a large mixing bowl and set aside.
2. In a microwave-safe bowl or stovetop, melt your coconut butter with your sticky sweetener of choice. Pour into the dry mixture and mix until well combined. Transfer to a lined 8 x 8-inch pan and press firmly in place. Freeze for 20-30 minutes or until firm.
3. Once firm, use a slightly wet, sharp knife and slice into 20 bars. Melt your chocolate chips of choice. Moving quickly, use two forks to dip each cherry coconut bar in the melted chocolate and ensure it is evenly coated. Repeat the process and refrigerate until the chocolate is firm.

Coconut Orange Creamsicle Fat Bombs

Serving Portions: 10
Total Prep Time: 10 minutes + freeze time (2-3 hours)
Macro Nutrients Each Serving:
- Carbs (net): 0.95 grams
- Calorie Amount: 177
- Protein Counts: 1.01 grams
- Fat Content (total): 19 grams

Essential Ingredients:
- Coconut oil (.5 cup)
- Cream cheese (4 oz./110 g)
- Heavy whipping cream (.5 cup)
- Liquid stevia (10 drops)
- MiO Orange Vanilla** (1 tsp.)
- Also Needed: Immersion blender & Silicone tray

Preparation Steps:
1. Blend all of the ingredients in a mixing container. If the mixture is too stiff, microwave it for a couple of seconds.
2. Spread the fixings into the tray and freeze for about two to three hours.
3. Once it's hardened, transfer to a container and store in the freezer until desired.
4. Note: ** The MiO can be found at stores including Walmart, Target, or Amazon.

Frozen Fat Bombs

Serving Portions: 10
Total Prep Time: 5 minutes + chill time
Macro Nutrients Each Serving:
- Carbs (net): 1.4 grams
- Calorie Amount: 185
- Protein Counts: 9.2 grams
- Fat Content (total): 28.7 grams

Essential Ingredients:
- Stevia (15 drops)
- Swerve (2 tbsp.)
- Cayenne pepper (.25 tsp.)
- Cocoa powder (2 tbsp.)
- Cinnamon (1 tsp.)
- Vanilla extract (1 tsp.)
- Coconut milk (1 cup)

Preparation Steps:
1. Start by making sure your oven is heated to 400° Fahrenheit/204° Celsius.
2. Warm the coconut milk for 20 seconds in a microwave-safe container.
3. Mix in the rest of the fixings - stir well.
4. Add the results to an ice cube tray and let it freeze for two hours.

Walnut Orange Chocolate Bombs

Serving Portions: 8
Total Prep Time: 10-15 minutes + chill time
Macro Nutrients Each Serving:
- Carbs (net): 2 grams
- Calorie Amount: 87
- Protein Counts: 2 grams
- Fat Content (total): 9 grams

Essential Ingredients:
- 85% Cocoa dark chocolate (12.5 grams/0.4 oz)
- Coconut oil - ex. virgin (.25 cup)
- Orange peel or orange extract (.5 tbsp.)
- Walnuts (1.75 cups)
- Cinnamon (1 tsp.)
- Stevia (10-15 drops)

Preparation Steps:
1. Melt the chocolate in a saucepan or the microwave. Add cinnamon and coconut oil. Sweeten mixture with stevia.
2. Grate the orange peel (if using). Then, chop and add the walnuts and orange peel.
3. In a muffin tin or a candy mold, spoon in the mixture.
4. Place in the refrigerator for one to three hours until the mixture is solid.

White Chocolate Fat Bomb

Serving Portions: 8
Total Prep Time: 1 hour 10 minutes
Macro Nutrients Each Serving:
- Carbs (net): 0.3 grams
- Calorie Amount: 265
- Protein Counts: 0.9 grams
- Fat Content (total): 20 grams

Essential Ingredients:
- Erythritol (4 tbsp. powdered)
- Butter (4 tbsp.)
- Coconut oil (4 tbsp.)
- Cocoa butter (4 oz./110 g)
- Chopped walnuts (.5 cup)
- Vanilla extract (.5 tsp.)
- Salt (.25 tsp)

Preparation Steps:
1. Prepare a pan using a medium-high temperature setting on the stovetop. Add the butter, coconut oil, and cocoa butter.
2. Once it's melted, add the walnuts, salt, stevia, vanilla extract, and erythritol. Mix well.
3. Pour into the silicone mold. Store the treats in the refrigerator for one hour before serving.

Chapter 8: Conclusion: Tips to Survive

I hope you have enjoyed each segment of the *Keto Vegetarian Cookbook*; let's hope it was informative and provided you with all of the tools you need to achieve your goals - whatever they may be. I will give you a few more clues on how to be successful with your new way of eating!

One of the easiest ways to stay on your chosen keto/intermittent fasting plan is to remove the temptations. Remove the chocolate, candy, bread, and sugary sodas you have stocked in your kitchen. If you live alone, it is one of the simplest of tasks. It is a little more challenging if you have a family.

Save Additional Carbohydrates:

- *Mashed Potatoes*: There's no need to prepare bowls of regular mashed potatoes. Instead, enjoy some mashed cauliflower.
- *Pasta*: Replace pasta using zucchini. Use a spiralizer and make long ribbons to cover your plate. It is excellent for many dishes served this way. You can also prepare spaghetti squash for regular spaghetti.

- *French Fries*: Change over to zucchini fries or turnip fries.

- *Tortillas*: Get ready, push this one to the side since it weighs approximately 98 grams for just one serving. Instead, enjoy a lettuce leaf for about one gram per serving.

Calm Your Cravings:

- *Sugary Foods:* Several things can trigger the desire for sugar, but typically phosphorous, and tryptophan are the culprits. Have a portion of cheese, cauliflower, or broccoli.

- *Fatty or Oily Foods:* The calcium and chloride levels need repair with some spinach, broccoli, or cheese.

- *Salty Foods:* Your body is craving silicon. Have a few nuts and seeds; just be sure to count them into your daily counts.

- *Chocolate*: The carbon, magnesium, and chromium levels are requesting a portion of spinach, nuts, and seeds, or some broccoli and cheese.

Now you can make the final preparations. The next step is to prepare a shopping list and head to the market!

"Don't go yet...there is one last thing to do. I hope you enjoyed the recipes and have started experiencing the benefits of a keto vegetarian diet. I would be grateful if you could leave a quick Amazon review. I know your time is important and for this reason even just a rating is highly appreciated. Your feedback can help us to improve the book. Thank you"

OTHER BOOK BY ZOEY BREANA RIMMER

PEGAN DIET COOKBOOK: The ultimate guide for beginners to improving health, losing extra weight and changing your long-term lifestyle with the pegan diet(basics, 50 recipes and a handy shopping list)

https://www.amazon.com/dp/B09BRF199P

INTERMITTENT FASTING FOR WOMEN OVER 50: An easy guide to burning stubborn fat and delaying aging with 200 delicious recipes

https://www.amazon.com/dp/B097FB3ZZW

Made in the USA
Monee, IL
05 March 2022